D0714499

I'M FINE!

Learning to Unblock Your Emotions

Dr Andrew Tresidder

Newleaf

Newleaf
an imprint of
Gill & Macmillan Ltd
Hume Avenue, Park West
Dublin 12
with associated companies throughout the world
www.gillmacmillan.ie

© Dr Andrew Tresidder 2002
0 7171 3416 4

Index by Susan Williams
Print origination in Ireland by Redbarn Publishing
Printed by ColourBooks Ltd, Dublin

This book is typeset in Sabon 10.5 on 16 point

The paper used in this book is made from the wood pulp of managed forests. For every tree felled, at least one tree is planted, thereby renewing natural resources.

A CIP catalogue record for this book is available
from the British Library.

1 3 5 4 2

Contents

Dedication

For Hilary, Frances, Isabel, Rose and Mum

Preface

Life is a journey with lots of experiences. In fact, life IS a journey of experiences!

Everything from standing and walking, reading and writing, to singing, playing music, riding a bike, using money, working computers, driving a car, eating a meal and everything else in the physical world.

At the same time we experience an invisible world of emotions – in fact, every aspect of our lives is coloured by our feelings and emotions. The vast majority of them resolve without problems – like the emotion that accompanies cleaning your teeth! But we get stuck on the big ones – and sometimes small ones. Why?

Only because nobody has ever given us a map to help us, and taught us the skills to use so we don't get stuck! After all, when a child falls off its bike, we pick it up and encourage it to have another go. But if someone is nasty to us many of us will choose to be nasty back. And the result? As Hardy said to Laurel, 'Here's another fine mess you've gotten us into!'

So this book is about the map we all deserve to know, and about our shadows (the suitcases of unresolved experiences we all carry around with us), and what we might find inside them – like blots, stains, tangles and cobwebs! And finally, it's about some of the tools we can use to help us resolve some of the baggage we're all lugging around.

Relax! – none of this is actually unfamiliar – in fact we all know much of it already – but it helps to have it explained.

Because, once it's explained and we've put on our safety belts, learnt the Highway Code, and had a driving lesson or two, and we use a map, we're much more likely to complete the journey safely and enjoyably – and get the most from it!

So – are you sitting comfortably? Then we'll begin!

Acknowledgments

I am indebted to everyone who has helped me understand what this book is trying to share. Particular thanks are due to everyone who has kindly allowed their stories to be retold, and to those who have written accounts and allowed them to be printed, especially Trisha Bailey, Becky Gillam, Diana Saunders and Joy Pike.

My deepest gratitude is due to Jannet Unite Penny, not only for her teaching and her essences, but particularly for most generously allowing me to quote in detail from her superb explanation of our Shadow. It would have been impossible to do the subject justice without her most kind gesture. I look forward very much to her book on the South African Flower Essences and our Shadow.

My great thanks to Daphne Moray, who has kindly typed most of the script from my typical doctor's handwriting, and especially to Michael Gill and all at Gill & Macmillan.

My heartfelt thanks to Hilary, Frances, Isabel and Rose and all my family for being there.

And a great thank you to all my friends for their loving support and encouragement.

Introduction

Emotional Well-Being – Healing Our Emotions

This book will help you understand the world of emotions, **the Emotional Broken Glass** that we all carry, and help you begin to deal with it painlessly. It will also look at some of the physical factors that affect our well-being.

Our emotional health is a major factor in our well-being, along with a healthy environment and healthy nutrition for our physical bodies.

There are guidelines and a sound body of 'common-sense' knowledge that enable us to choose sensible nutrition and use our environment wisely and safely – such as driving on the correct side of the road, wearing safety belts and so on. But when it comes to our emotions, nobody teaches us guidelines, and there are no maps available. We just pick it up as we go along, sometimes doing it well, sometimes less well, sometimes – well . . .!

In fact, because you can't see emotions, only their effects, there is an understandable temptation to ignore them, to keep a 'Stiff Upper Lip'! However, emotions not only exist – they are infectious too! If you don't believe me, just think of a crowded warm room in which one person yawns. What happens next? The yawn travels right around the room! Emotions act in the same way. But precisely because you can't see emotions, it's easy to deny their existence, or at least not acknowledge their presence, and their need for resolution.

As a result of the lack of a map, we are a bit at sea in this emotional fog, especially when the emotions are intense ones. In many societies, particularly Britain, expressing your emotions is frowned upon, and so children learn to bury, hide or deny their emotions. Young children haven't yet learnt this, so they cry, gurgle, smile and so on, completely spontaneously. But during childhood, we all learn not to be spontaneous, and so shut down our expression of ourselves as beings with emotions. The 'Can'ts', 'Mustn'ts' and 'Shouldn'ts' of life weigh heavily on our shoulders. With the shutting down of our expression of ourselves, we lose our coping strategies.

In losing our coping strategies for emotions, we become cluttered with years of dysfunctional unresolved emotional baggage – Emotional Broken Glass. We hope that 'time will heal' it – and it may do, slowly. We know that 'boys don't cry' – so that's one coping mechanism denied to half of society already! So the Emotional Broken Glass is buried, hidden, postponed, or even thrown at someone else. Babies don't carry Emotional Broken Glass – but most adults do! But to acknowledge the unresolved emotion is to start to experience pain again, so most of us deny it, or bury our pain.

The cost of not dealing proactively to resolve pent-up emotional stress is seen widely in life, its after-effects ranging from frustration to anger, to violence, to alcoholic obliteration, to broken homes and domestic violence, and subsequently reflected in the behaviour of children and partners.

Yet, in reality, if the maps that outline the process of resolving these emotions safely are explained to us, and the basic techniques remembered, then we can stop accumulating debris, and even start to deal with the backlog piled up in our personal in-tray.

Emotions accompany every experience we have as humans, be it common events such as getting up, making breakfast, queuing in a traffic jam, or the major ones such as bereavements, family break-ups and the like. Some are easy to deal with, others more difficult. Perhaps the point of emotions is to experience them, whether they be pleasurable or painful, to move through them and then to integrate the experience into our being, our personality. This way we see we can gain wisdom from the healthy resolution of our experiences and emotions. Blocking their resolution, however, prevents us from integrating the experience, painfully trapped as it is, in limbo. Perhaps the point of life is to have experiences, to accept them, to give them meaning, and then to move on. We cannot do this if the experience is clouded in unresolved issues.

Let's just look at three types of events in life, each of which carries emotion – for every single event in life is associated with emotion, however minor or trivial. In our lives we experience literally billions of emotions, the vast majority of which resolve spontaneously, unnoticed and invisible. When you clean your teeth, for example, there's not too much emotion attached – unless you lose the toothbrush and you're in a hurry, of course. However, this minor irritation will quickly subside. Going shopping on a busy Saturday before Christmas brings its own special kind of emotions, which may well grow as you queue, and you queue, and you sit in a traffic jam. These emotions resolve, usually, over a little while – but they may need some help. Did anyone mention a gin and tonic? Or perhaps the irritation may get thrown at someone or something else! And then there are the big events in life: the job changes, the house moves, the relationship changes, the bereavements. The emotions associated with these can be big stuff, can be heavy, can take days, weeks, months or even years to resolve on their own, without help.

By emotional well-being, we don't mean the absence of strong emotions such as hatred, irritation, anger or frustration. All of these are important, but the problem arises when any emotion is repressed, or inappropriately expressed. We all carry frozen patterns of unresolved emotion from our past experiences that cast a shadow on our capacity to live and be happy in the present moment – the anger that flares up, the confidence that has evaporated and so on. And of course, we always think that it's everyone else who needs the help, not us!

Perhaps our first map might help at this point. We call it the **Ladder of Emotional Healing**.

The Ladder of Emotional Healing, or Resolution, is as follows:

* Accept
* Acknowledge
* Forgive (the event, the other person, and crucially, yourself)
* Release
* Move On

Let's apply this process to the example of our feelings at the death of a loved one.

First we don't believe it has happened. We are in denial and we have to climb onto the first rung – Acceptance.

Next we have to admit to ourselves that not only has the event happened, but that it has profound effects that we need to take note of, and integrate into our lives. This is the second rung – Acknowledge.

The big step comes next – that of Forgiveness. We have to release our anger and frustration at the event. We have to forgive the other person for dying, and we have to forgive ourselves for feeling as we do. It is this step that is so difficult, and many of us get stuck here. Instead we often project blame, either outward – 'It was the doctor's fault' – or inwards – 'If only I'd. . .'. The latter becomes guilt.

Once we've come this far, Release, the next rung, is a relatively easy one, but can still involve large amounts of sadness that might linger with some people for a long time.

The final step, Move On, follows on from Release, allowing us to integrate the now fully resolved emotional experience into our lives.

What seems to happen for many of us is that in at least some areas of our lives, we get stuck on the Ladder on one or other rung. Once stuck – because it was too painful, the time was not right, or for whatever reason – it is difficult to get moving again – so we become 'frozen' to one particular rung of the ladder. But by realising that there is such a Ladder, and that we are stuck, we have insight into our problems and are able to start moving again, or at least recognise our need to get started.

What strategies are there to help us get started again, to move towards the resolution of our emotional baggage? What coping mechanisms are there?

'A problem shared is a problem halved'. **Talking** can help. Just the sharing of the story of an experience can, by articulating and clarifying it, give meaning to it, and help start the process towards resolution. This could be with a friend, a stranger (it's easier sometimes to share our secrets with a stranger than a friend) or a counsellor. It could include goal-setting or a problem-orientated approach. Counselling, of course, includes these techniques

The powerful technique of **Emotional Stress Release,** or **Rapid Memory Healing** is vital for us all to be able to access at will. Remember how people under stress sometimes put their hands on their forehead? This activates an emotional resolving process and can powerfully dissolve present problems, as well as buried past trauma, which may otherwise be contributing to flashbacks or feeling of panic. Of course, **tears,** even without a hand on the forehead, are a valuable release. Deep breathing can be harnessed in special techniques such as **Transformational Breathing**.

Touch is a very reassuring and helpful mechanism to help us feel secure, and support us in a safe place whilst resolution occurs. A hug is something every mother instinctively gives her child when it is distressed, unless she herself is feeling very unloved. Playing with an animal or child can also be cathartic.

Sometimes, however, the patterns of frozen emotion are held deep within us, often unconsciously. This brings its own problems, as Dr Dean Ornish's work in the USA has shown that expressing emotions and achieving emotional balance helps you live longer and more healthily. Such deeply held emotions can sometimes be uncovered by skilled counselling, or, quietly alone, by proactive use of the Emotional Stress Release technique.

Deeply held emotions may need another catalyst to start them moving on the ladder again, such as **Flower Essence Therapy** or **Homeopathy**. For instance, Rescue Remedy helps most people with acute distress and worry, whilst deeply held grief can be moved on and resolved by Ignatia, Natrum Mur, Staphisagria or others depending on the precise symptoms of the individual. The elements of Flower Essence Therapy and Emotional Stress Release are not difficult to master, and are already being taught more and more widely. Flower essences can be used over time, or in a sequential healing process to resolve specific blockages.

Sometimes pharmaceutical medicines may help us cope for a while if we are too deep in the pit of despair. They may work to lift our mood, whilst waiting for time to heal the deeper causes of the imbalance. Antidepressant use can certainly be life-saving, as before the introduction of ECT and modern antidepressants, many people tragically took their lives whilst in the throes of untreated and often unrecognised depression. However, the effects and addictive potential of diazepam, widely prescribed in the 1960s and 1970s, should not be forgotten. Initially hoped to be a magical cure for distress, it later became obvious that it did not resolve the causes of the distress. Worse, in some people the long-term use of diazepam was associated with an addiction syndrome, and a change in brain chemistry that only slowly reversed after stopping its use.

Alcohol should be mentioned, because it 'wipes clean' the emotional state but doesn't resolve or integrate the underlying experience. Rather, it acts to obliterate and distract our senses, just as excessive use of TV can also provide a distraction, so leading to a log-jam of unresolved issues.

Smoking is an often used release habit for emotional tension for many adults, just as sucking the thumb is for children, and sucking the breast or a dummy is for babies. It provides a form of security, but unfortunately, smoking is not at all safe! Most people in a traffic jam fiddle with their faces and mouths. Sucking a cigarette, or a pen, is merely a development of this. Drugs, as well as alcohol, are sought by many as a release from emotional stress or the pain and lack of meaning that life holds for them. Again, unfortunately, relief is short-lived, and only postpones any healthy resolution of emotions.

Emotional well-being is something we'd all like. Each of us is capable of creating a life to reflect the true expression of our heart's longing. This life is just waiting for us to live it – but to stay true to the perfect template, we need to listen carefully to, and act upon, the messages and feelings that flow towards us. These are often quiet whispers within us. At times the flow of these feelings and whispers gets blocked within us. Our emotions then go out of balance, and we become cluttered with emotional baggage which upsets our lives.

Yet the skills to help us with our emotions, and to live in balance, are not difficult to assimilate. A population strategy for emotional health does however require every single one of us to recognise the denial mechanism, unlock it, and be prepared to equip ourselves with the skills for emotional health. Then to teach the skills to as many others as possible, so that the habit of emotional healing is deeply ingrained in our culture.

After all, one of the challenges of life is to live in a way that enhances our self-worth and honours our self – 'that honours the unique, lovable, sacred and vastly capable being that we each are', as Tony Humphreys puts it in *Work and Worth*.

Perhaps the key issues are lack of knowledge about the journey of life and not having a map to show us what happens to our emotions, invisible as they are. So, without the tools to give us a detached view of life, we get caught up in strong and sticky emotions – and get stuck!

Let's explore these issues in the first two chapters! After all, you don't have to feel unwell to want to feel better.

Disclaimer

Whilst all the information in this book is given in good faith, neither the author nor the publisher is able to accept responsibility for the health of the reader or user. If you have any medical condition at all, please consult your medical adviser. In particular, if you suffer from depression or have any mental illness, please keep to the advice of your physician.

Visit Andrew Tresidder's website at www.dr-andrew-flowers.co.uk

CHAPTER 1

Life as a Journey – Emotions and All

THE RULES OF THE GAME

Just listen for a moment to the following exchange – a pleasant exchange, an exchange of pleasantries – heard thousands, if not millions of times every day up and down the country.

'How are you?'

'I'm fine, thanks. How are you?'

'I'm fine, thank you.'

What do we really mean when we say this?

As a doctor, if I walk down the streets of the town I practise in and ask anyone I know 'How are you?' it is treated as an invitation to a five-minute consultation, right here, right now, in the middle of the street. Very few people tell me they are 'Just fine' so I no longer ask this, unless I really want to know the answer! Instead, I greet people with 'Hope you're well', 'Nice to see you', or the like. Medical colleagues I know sometimes resort to looking straight ahead, avoiding eye contact, or assuming an expression of concentration that only the most insensitive person would wish to interrupt. A bit like most people act on the Underground in London.

Being a chatty friendly sort of person, I used to take pride in being able to engage strangers in conversation within just a few minutes of starting a train journey. I remember the shock I felt when I first travelled on the London Underground aged sixteen. It felt like a mortuary. All these people hiding their feelings and deliberately avoiding eye contact, or indeed any form of personal contact, as if they were afraid. And all I wanted to do was chat and make friends with one of life's fellow travellers, if only for a few pleasant minutes to pass the time of day. How naive I must have been! How insensitive, not to perceive the chains of fear, anxiety and worry that many people carry, and hide from themselves with a cloak of denial.

It is said that every morning certain races (perhaps the less spontaneous in the world's family) get up, get dressed and put on their masks. But all the same, to me, a sheltered country boy, on the Underground for the first time, this denial of feelings was a shock, one that even now I can remember.

How much greater the impact of regular shocks on a small, spontaneous, inquisitive, friendly child who keeps hearing the words 'No', 'You can't', 'You mustn't' and so on. So what does the child do each time it hears these words? It shuts down a little bit of its spontaneity, its warmth, its confidence. Gradually, as it makes its way uncertainly towards adulthood, it joins the rest of us in our shackles and chains, covered in layers of unexpressed emotion.

To return to the High Street of life, we all develop coping mechanisms to deal with emotions we are unable to express. Perhaps the problem is that it appears to be unacceptable to express your emotions freely, either at the time they occur, or shortly afterwards. What happens instead is that over the minutes, weeks and years, we build up layers and layers of blocked and stuck emotions. These layers handicap us, block our spontaneity, weigh us down and cost us a great deal of energy to maintain. Cost a great deal of energy to maintain? Yes, of course they do! Think of the energy we exert to keep smiling, to not swear, to put a brave face on things when what we really want to do is let rip, scream, laugh, swear, shout – whatever – in a word, to express honestly what we really do feel.

Back to the 'How are you? Fine' school of life. Perhaps 'Fine' stands for 'F.I.N.E', or Fearful, Insecure, Neurotic and Emotionally Imbalanced, as someone once told me. Why are people more honest with their doctor (or, perhaps, counsellor or other professional) than with their friends? Possibly we all say 'Fine' at times because it's not the right time to betray deeper feelings, or it's not the right person, or we have been conditioned that it's not OK to do so, or this is how we rationalise the world to ourselves. The trouble with this approach is that for most of us it becomes a habit, and we all end up using, to a greater or lesser extent, that most wonderful coping mechanism **Denial**. And that Denial becomes a habit, a habitual lie even to ourselves.

Again, there's a good explanation for the eminently sensible use that most of us make of Denial. Many things are just too painful to cope with at the time. Also, many of us find no safe place to express our feelings, or any person with whom to safely share them. And nobody teaches us the knowledge, skills and attitudes to deal with our feelings or emotions successfully. In fact, society is in denial about the emotional world – you can't see emotions, so they can't exist is how many people reason. Anyway, we tell ourselves that 'other people are worse off', that 'time heals all', that we need to keep a 'stiff upper lip' and encourage ourselves to bury deeper our unexpressed feelings. We're all victims together of a dysfunctional system that we all help to perpetuate.

And the end result? As Hardy said to Laurel, 'This is another fine mess you've got us into!' This is the mess that we all find ourselves in – and only we can get ourselves out.

How?

Well, life is a game, and we, including our emotions are very real players in the game. Do you think that if we could see emotions or knew how to resolve them we would be quite so careless with them?

How about, for a moment, looking at life from another perspective?

LIFE GAMES – UPSIDE DOWN: DRAFT PROPOSAL FOR A NEW APPROACH

Traditionally life's journey is approached from a position of a) ignorance b) being blindfolded and c) conditioned by society, family etc. to conform/be a victim/play certain roles.

We start out without knowing the purpose, the destination or the rules. A bit like starting a journey, blindfold, on horseback, not knowing it's a horse, not knowing how to ride, and not knowing either the best route or the destination.

So what do we do? We live in fear at one level at least, and take one step forwards, two to the side, two back, another forwards etc. All of which makes for a long, frightening and rather tedious journey, out of your personal control. Just like life for most people, in fact, unless they have luck on their side.

The trouble is that we all have responsibility or 'response-ability' – the ability to choose our own response to life's situations and challenges.

In fact this is part of the key to the answer – not such a sophisticated answer as the meaning of life, but at least how to get the most out of it. We often consider as irrelevant platitudes like

* Life is what you make it
* You get out what you put in
* Life's a bitch
* Smile and the world smiles with you

Actually they are all relevant – it's just that nobody tells you how or why. So we're all still stuck in a hole, simply because nobody has explained the rules or the purpose of life.

Perhaps, if for a pretend moment, we played life like this instead, with the following assumptions: (Ignore the ones you don't like.)

1. The purpose of life is to gain wisdom, experience of life's situations and to learn to love, whatever the circumstances or hardship. Our emotions are constantly with us, so part of the purpose is to accept and understand those emotions.

2. We choose to meet with a group of souls to share experiences to mutual benefit and gain. Not all experiences are pleasant – but we tend not to learn much by always having an easy time. All experiences are, however, opportunities to learn.

3. We attract to ourselves through the great Universal Law of Attraction whatever we consciously or subconsciously think about, be it pleasant or unpleasant, positive or negative. We also attract experiences through which we may learn, and so gain wisdom.

4. However, because nobody ever told us the rules of the game, we tend to keep mucking it up unless we are lucky.

5. Nobody ultimately judges us more accurately than we do ourselves.

The **Law of Emotional Healing** says that every action and event in life is attended by an emotional response, that the emotion is expressed in order to be experienced and that the purpose of the experience is to integrate that knowledge and feeling into our being. For the healthy resolution and integration of each emotion, it must be first accepted, second acknowledged, then forgiven and understood, before the next stage, release of the hold the emotion has on us. Finally we are then free to move on, having integrated the emotion into our experience of life.

Let's just repeat the Ladder of Emotional Healing again:

* Accept
* Acknowledge
* Forgive

* Release
* Move On

Remember that forgiveness can be difficult, especially for a bereavement, a divorce, or any form of separation. You have to forgive (understand) in three ways – the other person, the event, and yourself, for the way you feel. The inner child within each of us has the capacity to hold feelings of hurt for many years after a painful event, as I only realised on the twentieth anniversary of my father's sudden death. The inner child uncritically remembers many, many events and the unresolved emotions and issues that are painfully remembered or thankfully forgotten by the adult self.

In fact, the whole process has to be three-fold, covering event, the outside, and the inside. Since we always take things personally, and tend to focus on people, we rationalise issues as being about other people. In fact, it's much easier to see other people as being the problem in life's plots, than it is to accept our own responsibility. How often do we hear 'It's your fault!' and 'Look what you've made me do!'

The capacity of each one of us for self-justification is only exceeded by our ability to keep drawing breath! Let's just look at that another way – our ability to justify ourselves and our actions is so powerful that we only admit our mistakes when we choose to!

Bob was fifty-four years old. After a successful career in the Army, he'd worked in business as a Sales Director, which involved much travelling and staying away all week. The pressure took its toll. After a series of long journeys, Bob had a heart attack, which was his body's way of saying 'Enough –

stop!' Life slowed him down. Fortunately, Bob has made a full recovery. During his convalescence, he said to me something that struck a deep chord within me. What he said, was: 'It's only afterwards that you realise you've been an idiot.'

Knowing and appreciating our limitations, looking forwards, not rushing to overtake yet another lorry when the journey's end is near, is something nobody teaches us. But it's probably better to try and work it out, to travel life's journey safely.

It's only too easy to be wise after the event – the challenge is to be wise before and during it too – then we stand a chance of not ending up in another of Laurel and Hardy's fine messes! Awareness is part of the key – awareness on all levels, seeing the whole picture. And if awareness is important, so is balance. Emotional imbalance can so often lead us into problems – we may lose our temper, be upset, and then act out of balance. Like overtaking yet another lorry, because we feel in a rush, in a hurry, anxious or impatient. And then, halfway past the lorry, finding ourselves wishing we hadn't.

If we ignore the subtle messages of imbalance, the situation may continue to get worse, and may end in catastrophe.

Simon is a capable salesman but was working excessive hours at a gruelling pace a while back. Many people in Simon's position might be using alcohol or drugs as support. Simon wasn't. I saw him when he had a minor illness, and told him how in life we get subtle messages about being out of balance, tailoring my story to suit his situation of working far too hard.

The first messages we get are soft inner whispers that all is not well. We override them, choosing to ignore them. The next message may be a word from a stranger, or a phrase we notice in a paper. Too busy to be aware that this message is relevant to us, we plough on, set on our course. Our colleagues may comment, 'When did you last have a day off?' We ignore them. Sometimes the structure of work, with targets to achieve, bosses keen to meet deadlines, means that the messages we do listen to only serve to keep us on the same self-destructive course. Sometimes we are addicted to the adrenaline flow, or the external approval that comes with achievement – another factor that keeps us off balance.

Messages become less subtle: a cold that we work through, illness at the weekend or on holiday (a classic sign of long-term unhealthy imbalance). Our partner tells us there's a problem – we ignore them, or justify ourselves ever more forcefully. The children ask 'Where is Daddy (or Mummy)?' and eventually 'Who is Daddy?' Through all of this, were we able to look at a mirror of our emotions, we would see a picture of worsening imbalance, and would take steps to correct it. If it were someone else, we would be only too quick to help them to understand their shortcomings – if they would listen! And if they wouldn't, if we cared for them, we would tell them ever more firmly, until either they listened or we realised the futility of trying in an impossible situation.

But as it is our self that is at the centre of the stage, we often fail to listen to the messages until it is too late. As I told Simon, the next message is flu, which we work through, and then, if we still don't listen, life deals us a broken bone. Finally, I said, 'they' (it's easier to say 'they' than to acknowledge that we attract life's experiences to ourselves) resort to running us over with a bus.

Simon went off for the weekend. I was a little shaken to hear that the very next working day he had been in an accident which wrote off his car, and fractured his wrist. The chickens came home to roost with a rather chilling speed. Fortunately, Simon is now well, and very in balance – and listening carefully!

It is only by being aware, by listening carefully, that we can hope to keep in balance. And awareness of any emotional imbalance is central to being able to resolve it, and rebalance ourselves – for if we don't take action, life most certainly will!

So, when trapped in the dysfunctional patterns of life we all find ourselves in, the way to break out, to transcend the game, is to rumble it, to learn the rules, and play by them, using tools to transform ourselves and our emotions as part of the journey of life.

After all, none of us would set out on a journey of some distance barefoot or thinly clad, with no provisions or map, when the alternative could be a ride in a car, with map, food and fuel to make sure we got there, not just in the end, but in good time and in comfort.

One non-judgmental way we can help ourselves is by listening carefully, by being in emotional balance, and by conversation with others. We can gently review life's events and our position, saying first what we did well, then allowing others to say what they think we did well. The next step is for us to say what we think we could have done better. The final step is for the others to say what they feel we could have done better (and for us to listen and take notice of what they say!)

Negative criticism so often blocks people's ears – they rapidly become deaf and immune to it even when it is intended to help. You might say that the biggest temporary cause of deafness is not wax in the ears but emotional deafness! For so often, deep within we feel insecure – a very uncomfortable feeling. Being criticised resonates with this feeling and so we react by shutting ourselves off and not listening (internalising it) or by hitting out (externalising it).

Life could be better lived and learnt from, but instead we criticise each other too often instead of offering the loving support that we would all wish to receive. The path in front of us is so often obscured by fog, or FOG as Susan Forward calls it in *Emotional Blackmail* (Fear, Obligation and Guilt).

The Pain of Separation

Why this icy blast of criticism that stunts and withers so many of us emotionally, that handicaps and constrains us, and traps us into dysfunctional patterns of behaviour?

In this section we will look at the answers to these questions, the reasons why these patterns occur, and how we can start to lift ourselves out of the mess we find ourselves in.

It is said that no person deliberately makes a stupid decision when in full possession of all the facts about a situation. However, being in full possession of all the facts is not sufficient: the person must understand their own personal biases, and the biases of all the other people and factors involved. Then, if the Aim is clear, the Factors are all understood, and all possible Courses of action are apparent, then it will be apparent that there is only one Plan that is best for all concerned.

This type of logical planning is unconsciously used by us all, and was delightfully taught to me by a charming, self-effacing retired Major-General using the acronym All Fools Can't Play – Aims, Factors, Course of Action, Plan. He was self-effacing and unpretentious in the way that only those people with profound inner faith and self-knowledge are, to the extent that when my mother, due to meet him, asked 'How shall I know you?' the reply was 'I'm short, bald, with hairy ears!' And he was too. He forgot to mention that he also had the most delightful twinkle in his eye, the sort that makes you feel comfortable and secure. (This profound inner faith and self-knowledge brings what Dr Steven Covey in *The Seven Habits of Highly Effective People* calls Primary Greatness, that strength of character and inner security which you *know* within you, rather than that which other people, with varying degrees of conviction, tell you. Tony Humphreys describes it in *Work and Worth* as Self-Worth.)

People with this primary greatness have profound inner security, springing from a deep faith in themselves and in the process of life. Dr Edward Bach, the founder of modern Flower Essence Therapy, had Primary Greatness. He thought deeply about our emotions, and what factors could keep us healthy. He also formulated a philosophy about the journey of life in a paper called 'Free Thyself'. His previous paper, delivered to medical colleagues was entitled 'Ye suffer from yourselves!' so presumably he employed a little more diplomacy when writing 'Free Thyself'! His thinking runs something like this:

1. Health is harmony of mind, body and spirit. We should aim to live with a free heart, untrammelled by cares and worries.

2. Every person needs a purpose, a reason for living.

3. Each person is a small part of the god-force, or God, on a journey on earth.

4. This journey on earth is here to be enjoyed to the full, whatever work we do.

5. There is always divine help for us at all times on the journey, especially if we stray from our path.

6. Our souls will guide us in every circumstance and every difficulty if only we still ourselves and listen to the little voice within.

7. When guided by our souls to follow our path we radiate happiness and perfect health.

8. The journey of life is one of experiences and challenges, the purpose of which is to gain wisdom.

If we wish to believe in some of these concepts, it is easier to feel supported in life, to feel connected to something rather greater than just human life, to feel part of all that is. It is when we feel supported and part of a greater plan that we feel connected. Connected, perhaps, to God, or to whatever we each conceive the god-force to be.

Let's just look back at three concepts we've discussed: Awareness, Balance and Connection.

To be aware, we have to listen to the subtle messages of life and look at ourselves as we really are. In doing this, we can bring ourselves to, and maintain, a state of balance. Then we can feel supported and connected.

Awareness, Balance and Connection – ABC. Easy, really, isn't it! Awareness, of course, goes hand-in-hand with alignment.

Sadly in life there is no quick fix or short cut to emotional well-being unless we understand a couple of things, things that we looked at briefly in the last section.

Health is harmony of mind, body and spirit, including our emotions and all our stored experiences and wisdom. In a world where as adults we believe only what we can see or touch, to fully accept this concept causes some problems, but then, our bias is that of the world we have assimilated, a world in denial regarding the emotions.

The world in denial? Why so? Well, it is generally easier to ignore your handicaps and deficiencies than work through and resolve them, especially if culture dictates that we all act this way. As Nelson famously said of the approaching enemy, with his telescope to his blind eye, 'I see no ships'. And to try and buck the trend and go it alone often wins you no friends. Many are the blighted and blocked careers of those in business, or scientific research who sought to be true to themselves and their beliefs against prevailing fashions or the trends of the time, even though, like Galileo, they had a point – such as the world being round, not flat. The point is that deep down most of us are very insecure, deeply fearful, and so cling to routine, to the familiar, even when it is outmoded, redundant or frankly painful or poisonous to ourselves.

Let's just repeat that. Deep down every one of us is governed at some point by insecurity to some extent. This insecurity comes from fear, fear of change, fear of being different, fear of being alone, fear of being wrong, fear of being unsupported.

Within our mind-body complex, each of us has a left brain and a right brain, each with their particular talents. Whether we are female or male, each of us is made up of a synthesis from each side of the brain, the right being the more feminine side. Right-brain talents are knowing, feeling, unconditional love, intuition and creativity in all their different possible manifestations. The left brain is the seat of reason, logic and decisive rational action. To live successfully we need to utilise the talents of both sides of our brain. Returning to the analogy of the man on horseback, blindfolded, with no concept of destination, the right brain will help define the correct destination, remove the blindfold, and remind him how to ride, whilst the left brain helps logical action to keep the journey on its way, calculates supplies needed and assesses progress.

A few centuries ago, the forces of power in male-dominated, left-brain society worked very hard to eliminate those with predominantly right-brain talents by mass persecution of 'witches'. These were people with feminine intuitive skills, often the wise women, the healers, nurturers of the villages. Witchcraft became a crime and the excuse for the murder of many innocents by drowning, burning, hanging, stoning and other methods.

Nowadays, we in 'civilised society' live in a predominantly materialist, rational world – though all of us have, lying dormant, tremendous capabilities allied to right-brain skills. For most of us these skills lie dormant, unless permitted to flourish in safe ways such as flower arranging, painting or music, because in childhood the education system and our peers encouraged us to develop our left brain and shut down the right. For instance, we all learnt our tables in maths, learnt to read, and learnt copious facts.

If we were caught after, say, six years old, day-dreaming (akin to meditation, and a very right-brain activity for mental refreshment, creativity and so on), what happened? We were told 'Stop day-dreaming, sit up straight and concentrate!' And in our current adult world there are so many distractions such as radio, computer, newspapers and television that we hardly ever have time to think because our attention is constantly engaged. It seems as though we have become diverted from the Quality of Being into a frantic accumulation of a Quantity of Doing.

Which is more important? The Quality of Being or the Quantity of Doing?

I suppose it depends on whether we think of ourselves as Human Beings or Human Doings. And perhaps to live merely as Doings, without gaining meaning from the journey of life, is similar to going on a train journey where the windows are blanked out, so no value can be taken from the journey itself.

Living predominantly in our left brains, with a constant mental chatter, we are effectively governed by our egos, and not by our intuitive knowing self which needs stillness for its faint whispers to be heard. We constrict the constant inflow of energy that animates us and works through us. Although there is always guidance available at all times in life from our intuition, or Inner Self, we each develop, or have use of, an ego. Or should I say, EGO?

However, this is where the problems really start! For the ego perceives itself as separate, separate from spirit, separate from other people, separate from love. In a word, self-important. Yet, by being separate, in its own thinking, from all that is eternal and supportive, the ego is desperately insecure and fearful of its own mortality.

Having created the separation, the blockage, the ego perceives itself as weak and powerless, or at least insecure. In order to placate, if only temporarily, this insecurity, the ego tries to steal power from others, hence starting a lifetime of games of manipulation in order to gain temporary importance at someone else's expense.

To be fair to the poor old ego, incarnation in a physical body must be a pretty traumatic experience, especially when it realises what sort of company it has ended up with! All of whom are in denial, of course, and all playing games of manipulation to try to satisfy *their* own insecurities!

In *The Celestine Prophecy*, James Redfield talks about the four different ways we can manipulate a situation or other people in order to steal power. This happens when we lose our connection with our inner source of divine energy. We attempt to seize power and control the situation.

The four types of control range from the passive to the active. Most passive is the 'Poor-Me', a stance when we try to manipulate another by making them feel guilty. A little more active is the 'Aloof' control drama, where we choose to be detached and disengaged, forcing the other person to probe and work at engaging with us, rather than just allowing a natural gentle human exchange to take place. The

'Interrogator' type is a person who finds fault and nitpicks, keeping other people off balance, and thereby gaining power. The fourth is the most aggressive stance, that of 'Intimidator', or should I say INTIMIDATOR! The Intimidator demands and gets control by using fear to manipulate others.

There is similarity here to Eric Berne's classifications as to how we react and gain 'strokes', or little bits of reassurance from others. It was Berne who expounded **Transactional Analysis** in *I'm OK, You're OK* and the classic *Games People Play*. He suggests that within each of us there is an Adult, a Parent and a Child. The Adult is the grown-up balanced persona, the Parent is the protective yet potentially bossy character, and the Child is the playful creative, yet sometimes dependent and manipulative aspect.

Between two persons, the transaction can be Adult to Adult. This is likely to be harmonious and most productive. It can also be Parent to Child, or vice versa, which is potentially much more contentious. In fact, one person choosing to act bossily in Parent mode can force the other into behaving in Child mode. We often see this with young teenagers, who act in quite adult fashion when with their peer group, yet revert to childishness when with their parents. The parents may of course deliberately or unintentionally be pushing the teenager into acting in Child mode. The potential situations are many, and familiar to most of us. Always, of course, we feel we are on the receiving end, never the giving!

One game Eric Berne describes is that of Rescuer-Victim. This is a common game, played out daily in millions of different scenarios. Classically, a problem has arisen for one party. So far, no game. If this person seeks help without any emotional manipulation, no game arises. However, the moment this person feels one down, insecurity can arise. And insecurity is a painful vacuum which seeks to be filled, by reassurance at the very least, and by large quantities of emotional gratification at most.

So if a person feeling insecure seeks help, it is quite possible that they will accidentally play victim, driven by internal unnoticed emotions. The person they ask for help may of course have their own emotional needs to fulfil, and may be gratifying them by taking a helping role. It is a great calling and privilege to help others, but on occasions there may just be an element of self-gratification involved. Of course, a hard game of Victim entices the other person to play Rescuer, and vice versa, in the same way that an Interrogator stance may bring about a Poor-Me feeling in another person.

Every therapist, be they doctor, nurse, complementary practitioner, psychotherapist, or even mother, has ended up playing Rescuer intentionally or accidentally on occasions – and some clients may play a hard game of Victim. That's OK – as long as we are aware that it's happening! Every therapist – and mother – can tell you of times when they were caught out and thrown off balance by somebody playing victim. And most of us have also experienced somebody trying to rescue us when we didn't really want help!

Now, we haven't really discussed anything we haven't personally come across in life, but we may not have been taught it formally. Much of what we learn in life is not formally taught, but it doesn't make it any less true.

After all, there are two types of truth: first the sort we learn to pass exams and be accepted, and second, the truth that we just know is true deep within us, whatever anyone else tries to tell us. It is up to each of us to weigh up and accept, or not, each thing that is offered to us, for we each have accepted that responsibility as part of the contract for enjoying a human experience.

It is a moot point as to whether we are human beings aspiring to a spiritual experience, or spiritual beings aiming to have a human experience. Most religions would outwardly proclaim the former, but the inner core of each would support the latter. As someone once said, religion is the politics of spirituality, for the basis of all true religion is to act as an enabling force for spirituality, not to take power over its followers.

To sum up, we are beings of spirit incarnated (Latin for in flesh), or trapped, in matter, along with clouds of emotions, both bright and dark. We come to the wonderful playground or university for developing souls called life on earth. The journey for each successive lifetime starts before the womb, encompasses birth, infancy, childhood, family and school life, or maybe street life, the home, workplace, factory, office, building site, retirement home, hospital and so on. It includes experiences of nature, the elements, food, drink, breathing, chemicals, poisons, colour, light and dark, music, and many other vibrations and forms. It may be an easy ride with plenty of support, both on earth and from the god-force, or it may include famine, war, all sorts of abuse – racial, sexual, emotional, mental, physical, cultural or intellectual – in fact, all sorts of challenges to make us feel separate, fearful and insecure. It may be a mixture of both.

All these scenarios are workshops for developing souls to learn the lessons of love, of wisdom, of separation, of being in physical form, and provide opportunities to transcend our emotional baggage. They also provide scenarios where unlimited experiences can be absorbed, sponge-like, into our personal libraries. If you doubt the bit about the sponge, just think about the woman whose friend asked how their house extension was getting on. 'It'll be all right once the blessed bricks arrive! Daddy said so!' answered her three-year-old daughter triumphantly, before she could say a word. Children are patently the archetypal sponges, just soaking up experiences.

So, the journey to emotional health has to be a process of healing, a process of learning about ourselves and our blockages, how we work emotionally, and what makes us tick. Many factors impact on health. To learn about them, if necessarily first-hand, but sometimes mercifully second-hand, is to truly enjoy the human journey to the full.

Perhaps the single key fact is that separation causes pain and fear. Fear is the main result of apparent separation from the supportive unconditional god-force, and can take many forms as the separation permeates out through the layers of personality and emotion. These forms include anxiety, hatred, worry, excessive enthusiasm, domination, sadness, clinging to old habits or outworn and outmoded perspectives, dreaminess, lack of mental clarity, and above all, fear of change.

Fear is the dark-room of our lives where we process the negatives, as someone said. And fear often springs from lack of knowledge, from ignorance. As children, we learn many skills in the visible, tangible, physical world. When we get stuck, there's always encouragement. If we fall off our bike, someone will help us back on. But in the invisible world of emotions and energies (whatever they may be), there is no map, no guide, no pattern, and no culture of unconditional support. So, if we stumble or fall, like as not, when we try to get up again, somebody may push us over! A bit like a child, struggling to get back onto its bike, and being pushed off again! Hardly fair or kind!

We've all had this – we felt angry and expressed it. Or we went out of balance in another way. And instead of helping us work through it, the other people around us took it personally, and reflected the emotion straight back at us, and got angry with us! They pushed us back off the bike! Or, they may have chosen to withdraw into their own shell, withdrawn support, and allowed us to perpetuate our own imbalance. The alternative, of course, is to be supportive – but so often we feel threatened by emotions, and don't know how to handle them, so we don't offer support.

Why not?

Because nobody ever taught us the **Map of Emotional Resolution!** And without a map, we are in unfamiliar territory, so we feel ill at ease with these invisible and seemingly unpredictable emotions.

So let's share this map together, the map that we always wanted but nobody ever gave us!

CHAPTER 2

The Map You Always Wanted, but Nobody Gave You

If you go on a journey without a clear sense of destination – and, of course, direction – then you get lost. A bit obvious, really. In the physical world, most of us are familiar with maps. They stop you getting lost. Yet there aren't any clear maps for our emotional world – so let's try and create one together, based on common sense and our experiences of life.

Let's start with life being a journey, a journey of experiences. And let's also say that each experience consists of an event and of our emotional reaction to it. How does that sound?

So, we start with

Life = Journey of Experiences
Experience = Event + Emotional Reaction

Of course, our emotional reaction consists not just of our own personal immediate reaction – such as pleasure, happiness, fear, disbelief and so on – but is also coloured by our past experiences, by family, tribal, and cultural beliefs and assumptions, and by the experience of being human. But, for the sake of simplicity, let's call our total reaction our Emotional Reaction.

Every day we experience thousands, possibly millions of events. In a lifetime, billions. And every single one has emotion or reaction attached to or accompanying it. In the vast majority of cases, the emotion resolves completely, spontaneously, unnoticed, and invisibly. Which often leads us to think that nothing has happened! Whilst in reality, a very successful train of events has processed like a well-oiled machine to completion. Unnoticed.

So far, pretty obvious, you may say. But it's the next bit that's the stumbling block. You see, one of the things about us human beings is that we all tend to take things for granted, especially when they go well, and even more so when they pass unnoticed. So, in taking something for granted, we tend to forget how it happened and the factors that helped a situation go well. Especially when how it worked was invisible. Now, emotions may be invisible, but they certainly exist. Have you ever been hit by anger or touched by love?

So what happens to the Emotional Reaction is crucial. There are only two possibilities. Either the emotional reaction is experienced, expressed then resolved – or it isn't! And, if it isn't, though the event passes, the emotional reaction remains unresolved.

And what happens to unresolved emotional reactions and outmoded ways of thinking? Well, they're all stored up, a bit like post, or email, that has arrived but not been opened, acted upon and filed or deleted. In fact, most of us have a huge in-tray of unresolved emotional business, or a large backpack of baggage. This comes from several places – not just from the present, but from much of our personal past, much of our family, tribal and cultural past (prejudices and the like) and from other times and other spaces. The in-tray of our unresolved issues, or our **Shadow,** to use another term, contains various items. These can be categorised as **Blots, Stains, Tangles** and **Cobwebs.** We'll come back to them later.

Let's now draw the next map.

The Map of Emotional Resolution

Emotional Reaction

Is either

Fully experienced

Expressed and Evaluated

and finally

Resolved

to be

Integrated into life's lesson

or

Incompletely Experienced (or not at all),

Repressed, denied, buried, distracted, avoided

then

Unresolved, placed into 'Shadow' to

Await future reprocessing

* Experience
* Express
* Resolve
* Integrate

There are also five steps in the detail of the processing that are worth remembering, as we looked at in the last chapter – Accept, Acknowledge, Forgive, Release and Move On. Do remember, the Forgiving has to be done three ways – the other person has to be forgiven, and the event – and, most importantly, yourself, for the way you feel, and for undergoing the experience.

* Accept
* Acknowledge
* Release
* Forgive
* Move On

Now, using the Map of Emotional Resolution is an unconscious automatic skill that we all possess. A small child trying to stand up for the first time, falls over, picks itself up, tries again, and sooner or later succeeds. In the same way, we each learn to work through the map, but sometimes we go up the ladder of Healthy Resolution and Integration – that is, we've learnt that particular lesson life offered us – and sometimes, without help, we slide down the snake of Unresolved Emotion into the mire.

Life generally offers the chance to resolve the emotion time and again. However, if it causes us fear, if it's too painful, or we don't like it, or the lesson sets us too many challenges at once, we tend to 'Pass' and wait for the next event in life to catch up with us. A bit like a child who decided not to bother to learn to stand or walk, because it was too painful! In fact, an unexpressed emotional tantrum! Fear is the dark-room where we develop the negatives of our life.

At any point, an unresolved issue can surface from our Shadow, from the past, and be available to be **Relived, Relieved,** and then transit the **Experience, Express, Resolve** and **Integrate** sequence. This happens especially if something triggers the memory of it.

Let's just emphasise this point, as it's such an important one. An issue can be

* Relived
* Relieved, and then
* Resolved

or, in detail

* (Re-)Experienced
* Expressed
* Resolved then
* Integrated

However, unless you have more support and emotional coping skills at the point you relive an unresolved issue, it is liable to fall back into your Shadow again.

Here's a short piece that illustrates Healthy Emotional Resolution, after a period of Repression and Denial. It shows how mutual support over shared unresolved pain can lead to a healthy resolution. Written for a class magazine by Becky Gillam whilst in her last year at Primary School, it gives us insight into the use of the Map of Emotional Resolution as an everyday tool.

'I was so sad when all of my closest friends left Chard School for good. My friend Frances and I were devastated. We were both keeping our feelings bottled up and it was killing us. We both knew how each other felt – extreme pain. We were pretending that everything was fine and we could cope, but as a matter of fact we couldn't. One night Frances rang me up at home and just burst into tears. I tried to reassure her but suddenly I started crying. I couldn't help myself. A whole ten minutes was spent just crying. We told each other how we felt, and we both realised how life is much better when everything is out in the open.'

Can you see the stages in that story? Let's just repeat it, putting them in.

'I was so sad when all of my closest friends left Chard School for good.'
* Experience = Event + Emotion.

'My friend Frances and I were devastated.'
* Partial expression of painful Emotion.

'We were both keeping our feelings bottled up and it was killing us. We both knew how each other felt – extreme pain.'
* Emotion too intense, so placed into Shadow for later processing – but still causing pain.

'We were pretending that everything was fine and we could cope, but as a matter of fact we couldn't.'
* Repression and Denial – but the ice around the Shadow is pretty thin.

'One night Frances rang me up at home and just burst into tears.'
* Frances is reliving feelings surfacing out of Shadow.

'I tried to reassure her but suddenly I started crying.'
* Becky is unable to maintain denial and repression in the face of a resonant catalyst, which lifts the same, incident out of her own Shadow. Becky starts Reliving the Unresolved Emotion.

'I couldn't help myself. A whole ten minutes was spent just crying. We told each other how we felt, and we both realised how life is much better when everything is out in the open.'

＊ Emotion from both Frances' and Becky's Shadows is Relived, and so Relieved. This was able to happen at a time when both felt safe and supported. The Unresolved Emotion is Experienced, Expressed, Resolved and Integrated. Becky has even drawn for us the lesson from the whole experience – that life is much better when everything is out in the open, when the Shadow has released the experience, and when we have healed any outstanding issues and ourselves. Becky has elegantly illustrated the Map of Emotional Resolution to our advantage, as well as her own.

If we are not taught the Map of Emotional Resolution, we tend to take a healthy resolution for granted, and are hurt and surprised when we get stuck. But we all do from time to time, in various ways.

DENIAL

We all use **Denial** as a coping mechanism, this takes many forms such as **Repression,** when we bury it and pretend it's not there. **Distraction** – doing something else – and **Avoidance** are commonly used. My personal favourite is to bury myself into a newspaper when there's something to be done – or at least so my wife Hilary tells me! However, avoidance of small issues can easily develop into a major problem, such as if we experience a panic attack associated with a certain situation. Over time, this unresolved issue could grow and become a problem such as agoraphobia.

Projection is a bit more risky – this is when your unresolved emotion is triggered into coming up to the surface and you throw it at someone. This may not be the person who caused the original emotion – it's more likely to be the nearest person to you. Hence the reason why so often the messenger gets attacked for bringing bad news. 'Don't shoot the messenger!' What happens here is that the hearer of the message experiences emotion, and straightaway projects it toward the immediate source of the message – the messenger!

Comfort behaviour starts by sucking at the breast in infancy, moves on to sucking the bottle (a milk bottle, not the other sort!), sucking the thumb, sucking a pen, and then maybe sucking a cigarette.

Indeed, making yourself comfortable is an important coping mechanism – using such methods as smoking however are ill-advised.

Risk-taking behaviour such as driving too fast or having an illicit liaison is another way of distracting ourselves from our unresolved issues. Also, the adrenaline surge and excitement can give a buzz. This buzz can actually become addictive – many are the people addicted to adrenaline from one source or another. Curiously exercise, particularly if you get hot and sweaty, seems to burn off some unresolved emotion, such as exercising to release tension at the end of the day.

Escape into fantasy is a mechanism most of us love to indulge in at times – everybody loves a well-told story, and we all use our imaginations creatively from time to time. This equally can apply to the written story, or to the spoken.

Another coping mechanism is vitally important to understand – that of **Blotting it out** by substance abuse. One really effective way to forget your unresolved emotional pain has been used since time began – using alcohol or other drugs to forget about it. I suppose if I was a farm-worker out in the freezing fields a couple of hundred years ago, I'd have welcomed my gallon of cider a day! There's no doubt that substances from alcohol to nicotine, marijuana to cocaine, heroin to LSD all give a kick and a buzz (initially at least). But the long-term effects of using the quick chemical fix can be disastrous.

The last mechanism we use when there's just too much in our Shadow is **Overwhelm** – 'It's all too much' – manifesting in various methods of collapse, from nervous breakdown, to physical illness, and, as a tragic opt-out, suicide.

In summary, the mechanisms we use to avoid dealing with the contents of our Shadow are

* Repression
* Distraction
* Avoidance
* Projection
* Comfort behaviour
* Risk-taking behaviour
* Escape into fantasy
* Blotting it out
* And, if it's all too much, we can fall into Overwhelm and emotional Collapse

In *Why Men Don't Listen and Women Can't Read Maps*, a humorous yet serious look at the differences between male and female, Barbara and Allen Pease describe the coping mechanisms for unresolved emotional stuff like this:

Under pressure, men drink alcohol or invade another country – women eat chocolate or go shopping!

Let's look at these a moment, as coping mechanisms

Drinking alcohol is Blotting out the unresolved emotional pain. The quickest way I find at the end of a stressful day to unwind (the unresolved emotions) is to have a drink of alcohol. All the problems are instantly 'wiped' – or at least, my perception of them is. The trouble is, it makes me incapable of anything else and, even worse, the unfinished emotional business remains unfinished!

Invading another country is Projection: it is much easier to blame someone else for your problems, and divert attention, than take responsibility for yourself. My friend Jo hired a car on holiday abroad. After a particularly difficult stretch of road, she pulled up at a junction, only to be hit from behind. The man behind – another Englishman – stormed round to Jo's door, and shouted, 'You've been driving really badly. I've been following you for seven miles – and now look what you've made me do!' Look what YOU've made ME do! Fascinating, isn't it? Of course you and I have never used Projection, have we! No never! Well, hardly ever!

One interesting sophisticated development of Projection is that of role-playing for perverse gain – by which I mean not for a loving outcome, which is for the highest good of all parties. Dr Eric Berne in his delightful dissection of what makes us tick, *Games People Play*, talks about 'Life Games'.

Games such as 'Why Don't You', 'Yes But', and 'Wooden Leg' (I'd really like to do that, but I can't because of my wooden leg) are self-explanatory. Games can be played in the first, second or third degree, depending on how hard the player wants to play the game, and how gentle, or vicious, an outcome he or she is planning, or prepared to achieve.

One of the more extreme endings of a game is for one person to adopt a position such as Martyrdom. If metaphorical, such as when played in a kitchen drama between man and wife, it can be comical! And of course the deft use of humour can disarm and resolve a small issue quite easily. (Women, having greater emotional intelligence as a species, are often better at this than men – or so my wife keeps telling me! Mind you, when my mother first met Hilary, she did warn her not to tease me – obviously, I carried a fair amount of unresolved issues that made me feel vulnerable.)

If, on the other hand, Martyrdom is adopted by an individual or by a whole portion of society as a result of unresolved tension heaped upon unresolved tension, especially if those tensions have deep historical roots, the result can be catastrophic. One can end up with a society, or world, all stuck in a ghastly Lose-Lose situation. Anyone who has tried to separate two fighting dogs will tell you about it! Many wars are in part a playing out of the projection of unresolved emotion that stems from issues diplomacy has failed to deal with satisfactorily.

Asserting you own space is one thing, invading someone else's is different. Especially as most of us would rather be supported in resolving our own issues than have someone else shake us by the scruff of the neck – most of us then turn on the would-be helper!

Back to the allegedly female methods of avoiding dealing with our Shadow. Going shopping, of course, is both Distraction and Comfort behaviour rolled into one – and why not, you may ask? Better than hitting someone! Yes, but if you didn't have an unresolved issue to resolve, then you could use your energies for something more in tune with your life's purpose, rather than spending them avoiding it. Eating chocolate is also Comfort behaviour – and possibly Distraction.

And then there are the other ways of dealing with our Shadow. Repression is all too familiar to many, either in the family situation, at school, or subliminally in society. Repression is where we feel limited, and hold our emotions inside without expressing them. Many are the tears that are repressed, and the joys, for many of us. Men especially are constrained by 'Boys don't cry' and 'Keep a Stiff Upper Lip' – both powerful repressive dictums.

Risk-taking behaviour is one way of acting out to escape repression, but can occur on its own. Thrills include daring to push your personal limits, or challenging authority in all sorts of ways. It gets the adrenaline going, and brings excitement. This can include playing daredevil, flouting authority, driving cars too fast, and many forms of sport. Of course, the latter can be perfectly legitimate ways to spend time – but they can also be used for the secondary gain of thrills in order to avoid dealing with painful emotional baggage.

Escape into fantasy is another way of avoiding the issue – though of course, as with sport, listening to stories has held a deep fascination for human beings since ancient times. However, losing oneself in a fantasy world, whether of story, film, computer game or just the realms of imagination can, on occasion, serve to avoid important issues.

Finally, we all know the mechanism of Overwhelm and Collapse, when there's just too much to cope with. A seemingly trivial incident can bring about a breakdown, a collapse of the whole system. A single straw of extra emotional load can metaphorically break the camel's back, leading to overwhelm and exhaustion, or retreat into a mute state of numbness and inability to cope. It's not that the single final incident was strong enough to bring about the collapse – it is more that the house of cards needed only the slightest push to bring the whole structure down, because the coping mechanisms had already been saturated, and could now be overwhelmed with just a slight effort.

GAMES PEOPLE PLAY

Dr Eric Berne's book of this title deserves to be read by every therapist, every manager, every doctor and health professional, every father, every mother, and every young person. Dr Berne, an astute observer of human nature, maps out Transactional Analysis, and uncovers many of the life games that we can unconsciously play.

Each of us has three sides to our character, those of Adult, Parent and Child. The Adult is the wise, sensible, non-directive, balanced persona, the Parent the controlling, directing, guiding, sometimes overbearing or overprotective persona, whilst the Child is the spontaneous, playful, creative part that can also turn into a whining and manipulative being. We can play all or each of these roles from time to time, and can switch rapidly from one to another.

Every human being wants to be wanted, and needs 'Stroking' to receive emotional nutrition. Each interaction we have with another person can award strokes, or pats on the back. Strokes are essentially units of uplifting positive attention. Sometimes we give, or receive, negative strokes, or prods, which are units of negative attention. Humans thrive on strokes.

The most rewarding role to play out of Parent, Adult and Child, or at least the most profitable for our mature development, is Adult. If we are in Adult, then the other person is likely to be in Adult as well. If we are playing Parent, the other person, irrespective of age, may be forced into playing Child, whilst for one person to act as Child can make it likely that the other is pushed into playing Parent. You can imagine that Adult-Adult transactions are uplifting and developing for both parties. Parent-Child, and Child-Parent transactions are likely to involve stunted growth, and little room to manoeuvre, and inevitably involve energy theft by one or other party. The youngest son in one family spent a very grown-up evening with his parents at age eight. When asked why he wasn't like this all the time, he replied 'I don't get the attention if I don't play up, when my brothers are around!' You can see a game here!

Games are sometimes ways in which we play roles in order to steal attention and energy, even if the attention is negative.

Perversely, some people are attracted to the roles of Victim (forcing others into Rescuer) because of the internal lift it can give them. Victim-Rescuer is a classic game, played by many children (or adults acting the 'Child' role), and adopted unconsciously to a greater or lesser extent by anyone who takes the sick role. Victim equates to James Redfield's Poor-Me. At other times we may play Martyr 'Oh, don't worry about me, I'll be OK!' when really we feel desperately in need of support, help and attention.

Many of us unwittingly play one or more of Eric Berne's games as part of our life scripts. We cover over our pain by either retreating into hurt silence, or by projecting out a hostile prickly front. They say that bullies only bully because they hurt inside. And as Monty Roberts says, in *Horse Sense for People*, violence is for the violator, not for the victim. So unresolved inner emotions and issues can cause us to act out games in order to get some satisfaction and attention, even if it is of the negative kind. At times, attention of any sort is better than none at all – at least it distracts us from our own unresolved painful emotional issues.

This brings us back to the Map of Emotional Resolution. Let's look at it in more detail.

If you imagine an office, where post is received each day into the in-tray, dealt with on the desk, and then passed into the out-tray and automatically sent off, all goes smoothly when each item is dealt with in turn. However, if the owner of that desk decides not to deal with certain items in the in-tray they steadily accumulate, are unprocessed or not dealt with, and clog up the in-tray. The tray may become so full that the contents get moved elsewhere on the desk – and if unprocessed items still accumulate, then they are placed in piles on the floor. In fact, in the end, the room might end up looking a bit like my study used to – the result of too many bright ideas, none of them ever quite finished, and none of the filing done completely!

Through the journey of life, we consciously and unconsciously have many experiences. Especially as small children, we act like sponges picking up all sorts of experiences, vibes, prejudices and other thoughts without ever critically evaluating them. Many of these items pass effortlessly through the Process of Emotional Resolution with a healthy outcome but, for most of us, large amounts of issues, personal and cultural, tribal and family, get stacked up invisibly in piles around the desk, on the floor and elsewhere, cluttering up our unconscious mind and sometimes breaking through into conscious awareness.

Once an item has been pushed into the Shadows, a pattern of imbalance, or turbulence, has been created. No longer is everything in smooth harmony, but a blockage has been created in the flow of consciousness. And this process is repeated many, many times, so that most of us carry a large Shadow full of unresolved issues, full of Emotional Broken Glass, full of many little, and some major, patterns of imbalance.

Deny it or accept it, our Shadow is a part of each of us, held unconsciously and perhaps even lovingly, awaiting the time when we have the courage – and the map and the tools – to accept and resolve all the unresolved issues held there.

Why, you may ask, bother? Good question. After all, everyone else has got a big unresolved Shadow. If you're perfectly happy with life as it is, and have no desire to know what makes you tick at a deeper level, then leave your Shadow alone. But if you do want to pass Go and collect £200 (as in the game of Monopoly), if you are interested in using the maps we've just drawn together and if you want to use some easy tools to know yourself at a deeper level, and to resolve some of the unfinished business that you know about, as well as whole heaps of the stuff most of us are only dimly aware of, then let's carry on gently.

After all, inscribed on the famous Temple of Delphi in Ancient Greece were the words 'Know Yourself' and if that isn't an invitation to meet your Shadow, shake it by the hand and set about resolving it, I don't know what is. Incidentally, the other inscription at Delphi said 'Nothing in Excess', or 'Moderation in All Things'.

An old myth goes that the Gods were anxious that many should not discover the Secrets of the Universe too easily. In conference, one suggested placing them at the top of the highest mountain, another at the bottom of the deepest ocean. But Zeus, the King of the Gods, disagreed 'Surely man will be clever enough to search there – we must not make it too easy for him'. 'Where then shall we hide this great treasure?' asked another. 'Why, let us place it deep inside his heart – he will never think to search for it there!' replied Zeus. So perhaps the journey of self-discovery, of healing our Shadow, and of resolving patterns of imbalance has some use! Who knows what we might find if we have the courage to have a go?

EXPRESSING OUR EMOTIONS

Let's look for a moment at the healthy Expression of our emotions. We each have our own idiosyncrasies, our own personal ways of doing things. Expression involves allowing our feelings to come out from within, to be on the surface, and to flow. Babies do it, poets do it, singers do it, painters do it, musicians do it, dancers do it, potters do it, everyone in the world can do it. As the song goes, 'let's do it, let's fall in love' – which is where the answer lies, of course! For love as an undercurrent in our lives supports and maintains us. And when we feel supported, we are free to act with a light heart, spontaneously, without inhibition, and free from fear. As Kahlil Gibran puts it in *The Prophet*, 'Work is Love made manifest.' Expression involves one important concept – that of Living in the Moment. For when we are totally absorbed in what we are doing, we are fully living in the moment, not in our minds, neither in the future nor in the past, not in our hopes, nor in our fears.

And when we are supported and act spontaneously, living fully in the moment, we are free to be ourselves, to be Human Beings rather than Human Doings. As Dr Edward Bach put it, when we live according to the dictates of our souls, then we are free and can be our true Selves.

There are many ways of expressing ourselves emotionally and creatively. Exhibiting our emotions, with our body language, with our voices, in music, on paper, on canvas, or just normally as in everyday life, in human interactions or on our own, is just part of the Journey of Life. Sometimes emotional tension can grow too great – at this point, breathing slowly and counting to ten can be useful. Try telling that to a toddler! Toddlers have tantrums – in fact, a controlled tantrum, with a release of energy without a specific target can be quite beneficial, in the same way that a good thunderstorm clears the air from high electrical tension.

In fact, any build-up of emotional charge can be cleared by a rapid discharge, such as a flash of anger, a flush of ecstasy, a rush of creativity, a burst of laughter or a flood of tears. Each is cathartic in its way, clearing away the intensely felt emotion in a rapid flow of release. In fact, it is nigh on impossible to keep feeling an intensity of emotion without provoking a powerful Expression, leading to Resolution – it is when we block the flow of an emotion that we prevent a Release from happening. Creative expression deliberately using the emotions is how musicians, artists, writers, poets, dancers and others actually work, using the map of the emotions constructively.

Express, Experience, Resolve and Integrate. Accept, Acknowledge, Forgive, Release and Move On. There is one action, or rather activity, that is the synthesis of all these processes, and that is one we all take for granted. What is worse, we tend to undervalue it, or even ridicule it, because we are too busy. That activity, or process, is **Reflection**.

REFLECTION

Reflection is the process by which we take meaning from life's experiences.

It is in Reflection that we can weigh up an experience, we can measure its true worth, and can review any unresolved issues, be they events, possible outcomes that didn't happen, the way we handled the issue, and our emotional reaction to them.

Reflection is perhaps *the* key process that underpins our processing of life's experiences. It is in Reflection that we become aware of their significance on many levels. Reflection is the key to the healthy Resolution of life's experiences. For Reflection to happen, we need support, time, space, and a resonance to help us access the issue, all the while supported by a framework or scaffolding that enables us to catalyse a Resolution of the issue.

Reflection is something we do naturally as self-conscious human beings. In fact, it is by virtue of Reflection that we allow ourselves to be Human Beings and not Human Doings. If you're too busy doing, you often have no time to Reflect upon your Experiences. You have no opportunity to take meaning from the process of life, no way of being fully aware and gaining full value from each of life's events. And yet it's a process that is so easy, if we give ourselves the time and space to do it.

It is in Reflecting upon an issue that we can weigh it up. It is part of the process of reflecting for questions and regrets to come into our minds – thoughts such as 'What if?' and 'If only'. These are little helpful questions that are asked almost unconsciously, and answers received almost unconsciously, when we are in a state of emotional balance. We go shopping, our instincts tell us to buy baked beans, or fruit, or whatever, and we feel good. We've made the right decision almost unthinkingly, and, on reflection, it feels right.

But when we are out of balance, our judgment becomes clouded. The 'What Ifs' and the 'If Onlys' can come to conscious state and become almost irrational precisely because we are out of balance. This happens particularly if we have large amounts of strong emotion distracting or destabilising us. Let's just look at an example, one many health professionals will recognise, and one which we can each get caught up in at a personal level.

When a loved one dies, we may experience many strong emotions. We feel shock, we feel loss, we feel alone, we feel hurt, we feel cheated, we feel sad, and we feel guilty. All of these feelings wash through us, and more besides.

Over time, through the process of grieving, we can come to terms with all of these feelings. We Accept the bereavement, we Acknowledge it, we Forgive the death, we Forgive the loved one for passing over, we Forgive ourselves for the way we feel, we Release the experience, and we are free to Move On. We Experience, Express, Resolve and Integrate.

During this process, we feel many strong emotions. And, as I tell my patients, at times like this we are liable to be pestered by two unwanted families – the 'What Ifs' and the 'If Onlys'. If we are pestered when we are out of emotional balance, we can end up being sent down all sorts of blind alleys and led up the garden path. Classically, as I say to my bereaved patients, all sorts of questions will come up. 'What if he'd eaten a better diet?' 'What if he'd had one sugar in his tea instead of two?' 'If only I'd taken her only holiday this year.' These are all thoughts that can lead to emotion being directed against oneself, often as guilt.

There are also other sorts of questions, those that lead to unresolved emotion being directed against someone else – often as anger, often towards the medical or nursing professions for example. 'If only they'd found it earlier!' 'What if they had?' 'What if my children had come to visit us more often – this wouldn't have happened' 'If only they had been operated on sooner, been given chemotherapy or antibiotics, been in a better hospital!' It's not far from allowing these thoughts to fester to starting to believe them – in which case the death of a loved one becomes somebody else's fault.

Please, I'm not trying to trivialise this important issue, nor trying to put the litigation lawyers out of business. I'm only trying to remind all of us that strong emotions can throw our judgment and our peace of mind out of balance. And if you have a large quantity of raw, painful, unresolved emotion, it's often easier to internalise it (by guilt or self-blame), or externalise it (blaming someone else) than it is to pause, stand back, and make sure you are emotionally continent. And, having ensured that you are not about to be emotionally incontinent either over yourself or anyone else, to then Reflect and allow yourself to transit the Map of Emotional Resolution

TUNING FORKS AND RESONANCE

Tuning forks are metal objects that look like forks. When struck, they sound a note of precise harmonic pitch. You may remember from school the experiment with two tuning forks, both at the same pitch, situated at opposite ends of a large bare room. When one is set going, the other will pick up the resonance frequency and respond by sounding its own identical note. This phenomenon is called entrainment.

Let's look at tuning forks, especially those provided by nature. For nature always seems to maintain balance and harmony effortlessly. As someone once said, 'Consider the lilies of the field – do they toil and spin?' – or, as you might say today, do trees try to be trees? – do flowers try to be flowers? Of course not, they just are, they just do it!

Plants and simple sounds are all built on very precise mathematical principles. If you look at a flower, you can count a precise number of petals, of stamens and sepals, and these can be described precisely and mathematically. Well, they can by a mathematician, but you and I will probably just appreciate their beauty. The significance of this mathematical precision is that the 'essence' of the plant or flower is mathematically precise harmony, so when the signature of the flower is captured by an essence maker, a precise harmonic tuning fork for our emotions is produced and preserved, to be used at another time and in another place.

Because they are based on precise harmonic mathematical principles, flowers, sounds and colours all have their resonant signatures. Flower and other vibrational essences can act as tuning forks for our emotions, in the same way that a particular sound or colour can evoke a response in us.

There are many other tuning forks in nature. Just imagine gazing at waves gently rolling in on the seashore, or leaves wafting in the breeze, a beautiful garden, an uplifting landscape, or a wondrous sunset. All have the capacity to uplift and to inspire – and not just if you're a poet!

Tuning forks are catalysts for change, tools to help re-harmonise patterns of imbalance. Essentially, tuning forks produce harmonious wave forms, in sound if we can hear it, in light and colour if we can see it and in the whole vibrational spectrum, most of it undetectable by our five senses.

The Latin word *resonare* means to echo or resound, to send back an echo or to make something resound. Of course resonance applies primarily to sound, although the term is now used to talk about any vibration or vibe. The classic resonance is the echo from a cave, where your voice is not only echoed, but amplified as well.

Resonance is when something strikes a familiar chord. It resonates with something we already know or have met. It brings something back to mind. The right resonance can bring pleasurable memories to mind, a different one might remind us of someone or something that caused us pain in the past. This can bring emotion up to the surface from the past. Memories, stories, music, photographs, and of course, that modern story medium *par excellence*, films, are wonderful tools for stimulating our own personal issues and emotions to come to the surface, by offering patterns and emotions that we can resonate with.

The Law of Resonance states that if two objects vibrating at different frequencies are brought together, either the stronger frequency will entrain the other, or they will meet in the middle.

What is more, a harmonious note, such as a tuning fork, can entrain patterns of disharmony and reharmonise them if they are capable of resonating at this frequency.

Everything has its resonant note or vibration. Using the phenomenon of resonance, an opera singer can project her voice at the precise pitch at which a wineglass resonates. Amplifying this note can make the wineglass resonate and vibrate so forcefully that it can shatter. Interestingly, sound can have healing properties as well. We all know how some music can calm and make us feel better – the best example might be a mother singing a lullaby to her child. Curiously it seems that the human voice has particular healing ability – and, of course, the nasal cavity and the resonant chambers in the faces, the sinuses, create the particular resonance of the human voice.

Ancient cultures created underground chambers such as the Beehives of Ireland, which can resonate, echo and amplify certain sounds to the point where you can feel uplifted and changed – in a way, rebalanced. It seems that some ancient cultures understood more about healing vibes than we do!

In fact, the healing power of song is well known to us all from many favourite pieces of music. And many of us catch ourselves humming, singing or whistling when happy. It's likely that former generations used song regularly, even if unconsciously – think of all those Medieval paintings of open-mouthed peasants in galleries. Presumably they were singing and chanting. Remember the way in which grateful Medieval kings and knights would set up churches and chantries, so that choirs might chant and sing God's praises. These churches were often situated on ancient sacred sites, or places at least where the vibes already felt good.

Hardly surprising really – if you want to go out with a friend or loved one for a special occasion, you don't choose somewhere that feels grotty and yucky, do you? No. Naturally you choose a place that feels good, like the coast, a beauty spot or a nice welcoming venue! Unconsciously, what you are doing is seeking to use the naturally good vibes of particular places to resonate with your meeting, and tune yourself up a bit!

Resonance is also an important principle when it comes to our memories, particularly unresolved ones. These are the ones we keep stored in our invisible in-tray, in our Shadow.

The right resonance can bring an issue back out of our Shadow to start it reprocessing. This resonant trigger can be a sound, an experience, a piece of music, a colour, a similar dress, car, building, picture, film or any trigger that resonates with an unresolved buried memory. In essence, any sight, sound, smell, taste or feel can access our memory banks and resonate with a particular one that can then be brought to the surface. Even triggers such as situations, or times of year can act as triggers in most unexpected ways. Triggers can bring back negative unresolved issues, but they can also remind us of pleasant memories.

Let's look at a couple of examples:

On Remembrance Sunday 1999 I was wandering around the garden with my hand on my forehead. This is a powerful gesture that holds two kinesiology holding points, and seems to bring memories up to the surface for reliving, relieving and resolving. (The two points are the frontal eminences, for anatomy students, or where our horns would sprout from if we were cows. Holding them seems to make a circuit that facilitates the processing of emotion.

We'll look at the Emotional Stress Release technique in Keep Cleansing, Stay Grounded.)

Gradually I became aware of an unresolved issue surfacing from my Shadow. When this happens, I try to let a phrase or some words express the feelings. Articulating a story, whether to ourselves or to others, clarifies the issue and gives it meaning in our own minds. What came to the surface, gradually at first, then more firmly, was a strong feeling of loss. This became articulated as 'My Daddy's died, my Daddy's died, my Daddy's died'. This feeling came out together with unexpressed tears, upset and grief – though if you'd asked me, I'd have said I'd dealt with the issue years before. In fact, my father had died suddenly and unexpectedly exactly twenty years previously on Remembrance Sunday.

It seems that the trigger of a day of remembrance and mourning, at coincidentally the same time of year, had enabled me to access feelings of unresolved grief, not from the logical left side of my brain, but from the feeling right side, from the hurt Inner Child. And in bringing it to the surface, I could Relive and then Relieve the experience, leading into Experience, Express, Resolve and Integrate. Curiously, in thinking about this story, I remember feeling a change in my emotion, a resolution to the painful emotion, whilst standing under the walnut tree. Walnut in the Bach Flower Essence system is the Link-Breaker, the protector during times of change, and one of the key essences to be used at times of bereavement.

Let's just run over those stages again – Relive, allowing us to Relieve, then Experience, Express, Resolve and Integrate.

Relive, Relieve, Resolve and Integrate – the key to resolving past patterns of imbalance. Lesson now over and learnt!

The second resonance arose not so much from it being the same time of year as from the occurrence of a similar event, a generation on. Frances, my eldest daughter, was excited about starting at Secondary School. This was in contrast to my some of my own experiences of school, especially Primary. Aged eight, I had gone to boarding school some seventy miles from home. I was very unhappy. I am told that I cried every day of the first term. At the moment of leaving Frances at the bus stop on her first day, a huge sense of pain and loss overwhelmed me. I found myself first accessing, then articulating a frozen emotional pattern of 'I hate school, I hate school', accompanied by the shedding of tears. I recognised this as an opportunity to resolve a frozen pattern of imbalance. Some thirty-five years previously this pattern had cycled itself round and round in my psyche in circles of self-pity, eventually to be gathered up by the Shadow to be held and dealt with at a later date. Here now was the date, the pattern brought to the surface by the appropriate resonant trigger. Of course, I then had to do morning surgery at my Practice!

Fortunately, Nature's tuning forks are always at hand. A short stroll past several gardens brought me to a flower whose pattern of coherent energy acted as a tuning fork to help a resolution of the imbalanced state. And a few more essences from the set I keep by me helped to finally dispel the imbalance. In doing so, I found myself filled with compassion for all children who experience a similar separation, for myself for accepting the experience (in the end!), and especially for my parents. They had sent me to board, knowing it was for the best – but it must have caused them considerable pain and anxiety to observe, from afar, my unhappiness yet know that it was right to not interfere.

We've just looked at two unresolved issues that were deep in my own personal in-tray – unexpectedly brought to the surface by a seeming chance resonance. How much do we each carry in our own in-tray? And why is it there? Before we start beating ourselves up about what is unresolved, we should congratulate ourselves on all the millions and billions of things we have resolved! And we learnt to ride a bike, to drive a car, to use a phone, a computer, to express ourselves in many different ways.

In a way, having the skills and tools to deal with unresolved issues is not a problem, just a project. A project of learning a map, skills and tools to help us gain full benefit from each of life's experiences – to Experience, Express, Resolve and Integrate, making sure we are able to Accept, Acknowledge, Forgive, Release and Move On from each of life's opportunities or lessons. And then, we can Accept our lives, our experiences and our Selves with love, without judgment.

When each issue in the in-tray is dealt with in turn, when each issue is worked through and then Accepted, when we are able to live in the moment and act spontaneously, then we live in Flow, in harmony with the flow of our lives.

FLOW AND BLOCKAGE

Let's talk a little about Flow and Blockage, and introduce the concept of turbulence. Along with this will come Harmony and Disharmony.

Imagine a river, with banks, shallows, rapids, rocks, eddies and a slow current strongest in the centre of the stream. Picture now a boat on the river, carefully navigating downstream, working with the current. There are many difficulties and dangers for the careless helmsman, the incautious captain. It is easy for the boat to veer toward one bank or the other, to get stuck, or to run onto the shallows. It is also possible for the boat to hit rocks, to shoot the rapids too fast and overturn, or to be caught in an eddy, ending up pointing in the wrong direction and going nowhere fast. In order to make best use of the stream, and to gain the destination swiftly yet safely requires courage, wisdom and sound judgement.

If you use this analogy to describe how a government should act, you can see that nobody offers thanks to the government for doing the job well – just blame and criticism, often even if they get it right, but especially if they get it wrong. After all, the world is moving from a Blame Culture to an Appreciation Culture painfully slowly at times. It appears that gratitude, giving thanks, being satisfied with what we've got is quite a difficult habit to keep going. Why exactly that should be is explained by the mechanism of habituation – that is to say, getting used to something, and taking it for granted.

Habituation is getting used to something so you fail to notice it. It's something we all do. Say you get pocket money every time you see a favourite aunt. If you one day see her and she fails to give you something, it's easy to feel cheated! That's habituation and we end up taking things for granted, especially things like the weather, daylight, nature, food, shelter, company, friends – indeed anything.

You can apply the principle of navigation to Industry and Commerce, and see how managers really need to be good helmsmen, good captains – and perhaps also good 'Systems Doctors' – in order to get the best from, and for, their companies, colleagues and employees.

Now apply this analogy of the captain of the boat to yourself. Plenty of dangers and difficulties meet you on the journey of life – all opportunities to gain wisdom and experience – and nobody thanks for you for getting it right. But you receive plenty of blame and criticism if you get it wrong.

So how does the captain get it right? By using experience, wisdom, and often gut feeling – by listening to the little messages that come to him, often as quiet whispers. By calculating, evaluating, taking soundings, taking bearings, checking his position on the charts and above all by being alert for the first signs of disharmony and imbalance, for he knows that they may hint at hidden rocks or shallows. And then he acts carefully at the earliest hint that action might need to be taken. That way, the gentlest correction will often be sufficient to realign the boat to the best course.

So it is for us in our lives. If we listen to the subtle messages, to the gentlest hints that we find on our way, and act upon them early, then we avoid major problems. In addition, if we make sure our vessel is well maintained, has no leaks, no patterns of imbalance, and plenty of fuel, then we have the best chance of making the voyage to best advantage. Let's face it, the voyage of life is already underway – so let's make the best of it!

To return to the analogy of the river – the stream of the river is strong, and any barriers will create turbulence. However, in the short run or in the long run, the strength of the stream will erode a barrier – or at times sweep it away, whether or not the blockage likes it. For, in the natural order of things, all is either flow or blockage – and blockage is always temporary to a greater or lesser degree.

How does all this relate to our lives?

Well, firstly blockages and patterns of imbalance, will always meet with ever-increasing resistance, and pressure to resolve. It seems that there is a harmonising force in nature that wants to correct imbalances. And, secondly, it is worth listening to the subtlest hints as to correct navigation, before the failure to follow the hints results in a major blockage and turbulence – a pattern of imbalance.

And when you have a major pattern of imbalance, with forces still building up, sooner or later you end up with a crisis. This is just as true of a single person as it is of a family or a country.

If you take a small child with more and more unresolved issues – it may sink into withdrawal and depression – but it's far more likely to have a tantrum first! A tantrum is an explosive outburst that can dissipate and dissolve a large amount of unresolved anger or frustration, and it's a valuable mechanism to achieve that – as long as it's done in the right place, at the right time, and is channelled appropriately. Remember, anger is a powerful force that can actually be directed creatively – especially if humour can be involved!

And how do we keep in balance, stay in tune, remain in harmony and navigate the stream of life safely? How does a good band of musicians keep in time, in tune and play in harmony, especially when improvising? By tuning up carefully, by retuning as need be – on the move! – and by carefully going with the flow, each musician following their inspiration and intuition.

Finally, let's just recap on the key points of this chapter.

We can all be helped by a map of how our emotions flow – or get blocked. The map is very simple.

Life = Journey of Experiences
Experience = Event + Emotional Reaction

The Map of Emotional Resolution

Emotional Reaction

Is either

Fully experienced

Expressed and Evaluated

and finally

Resolved

to be

Integrated into life's lesson

or

Incompletely Experienced (or not at all),

Repressed, denied, buried, distracted, avoided

then

Unresolved, placed into 'Shadow' to

Await future reprocessing

* Experience
* Express
* Resolve
* Integrate

The mechanism we use to keep issues unprocessed and in our Shadow:

* Denial

The means we use to stay in Denial:

* Repression
* Distraction
* Avoidance
* Projection (outwards or internally)
* Comfort behaviour
* Risk-Taking behaviour
* Escape into fantasy
* Blotting it out
* and then when it all gets too much – Overwhelm.

Any Trigger can start an issue reprocessing, at which point we can either try to stop it processing, or we can try and find support to help us, At this point we can choose to

* Relive
* Relieve
* Re-experience
* Express
* Resolve
* Integrate

When our reaction to events is processed and resolved, it is Reflection that is the underlying process. Reflection is the process by which we take meaning from our life's experiences.

As each issue is Reflected upon, it is

* Accepted
* Acknowledged
* Forgiven and
* Released and then we are free to
* Move On

And to help us through the sequence are various tuning forks and techniques to rebalance ourselves. Before we can look at the tools to help rebalance, it's useful to look more closely at what makes up a Human Being. We'll do this in the next chapter, 'Conscious Energy – Good Vibes, Bad Vibes'.

CHAPTER 3

Conscious Energy – Good Vibes, Bad Vibes

What is it to be Human? Quite a big question, really! Now, I'm not going to lead you into any deep philosophical discussion, so please relax! What I do want to discuss are some of the things that we all know, but that we take for granted about being Human – because if we're aware of these factors, then we can know what drives us and what makes us tick.

One of the things we all take for granted is life – we expect to wake up each day, we expect food, we expect the sun to shine, the breeze to blow, and, if you live in England, the rain to fall!

We expect to be in our physical body, we expect to use it, we expect it to work, and we expect it to do what we want it to do.

We expect to be able to achieve what we intend to – whether it's climbing the stairs, brushing our teeth, driving a car, writing or reading, cooking, dancing, walking, or any of the many other things of which human bodies are capable.

These expectations, or assumptions, are part of our everyday life – we even take the assumptions for granted!

Yet behind every assumption are miracles! Turning a switch and seeing electric light seems like a miraculous process. The workings of cars and lorries, let alone aeroplanes, seem like miracles. The wheel, the internal combustion engine, the computer, email, and space travel all seem like miracles! Yet there is generally a rational scientific explanation for these happenings. Perhaps miracles are simply events whose mechanism is hidden?

WESTERN KNOWLEDGE OF BODY AND MIND

The Western orthodox tradition of science has made many astonishing advances for the benefit of mankind. In the last few centuries we've seen the rise of literacy, agricultural and transport revolutions, and, more recently information technology and communications revolutions. Each of these advances has sound rational explanations as to why and how they happened.

Similarly Western scientific investigation has discovered many of the details as to how our bodies work. In the field of human bodies and consciousness, research has enabled us to understand how electrical impulses in nerves make muscles move, how blood circulates around the body, how that flow of blood removes waste products whilst providing nutrients, how the lungs take up oxygen and release carbon dioxide, how the kidneys filter out waste products and how the liver produces metabolic energy. Research has more recently helped us comprehend how the brain works, and that little chemical compounds called neurotransmitters are found not just in the brain, but all around the body. It is the flow of these neurotransmitters that governs how we feel, whether we feel pleasure or pain, comfort or discomfort. It is due to the marvels of these neurotransmitters, that the body is able to repair itself if wounded, is able to marshal the immune system to combat and overcome foreign invaders like bacteria and viruses.

All neurotransmitters have roles. Adrenaline and cortisol are alerting and inflammation messengers. Some alertness and tension in the body is essential to enable us to react to threats and danger. Threats cause our bodies to produce adrenaline, cortisol and a host of other chemicals. In turn, these chemical messengers, adrenaline for example, cause the heart to pump more forcefully, tighten up some arteries, divert blood away from the skin and gut to let it flow to muscle instead, and make us more alert. Ready to run away from danger fast! Useful in the jungle, or playing football or sports. Not useful if you're sitting in a traffic jam. The tension just stays high in you without possibility of release by physical exercise. It is partly this unresolved pent-up tension that contributes to road-rage.

Cortisol is also vital. There is a disease called Addison's, where the body cannot produce enough cortisol. Replacement therapy helps people to live a normal life – but, if infection or trauma should happen, the body's normal response to quickly create large amounts of cortisol doesn't work. I remember going to see a normally fit thirty-five-year-old man who had diarrhoea and vomiting, something most children and adults get over quickly. Within an hour of the start of the illness, he had collapsed to the ground and was nearly unconscious. His blood pressure was low, and he was continuously being sick. An injection of synthetic cortisol into a vein was not only life-saving – it was little short of miraculous. Within minutes this man was sitting up, considerably better, and within hours he was back to normal. He did have an overnight stay in hospital, but it was the initial injection that had such a dramatic response.

There are other, more pleasurable neurotransmitters called endorphins, or endogenous morphine-like substances. Discovered by Dr Candace Pert, they are the body's own pleasure messengers, which flow through the body when we feel calm and relaxed, and especially when we feel good and happy. It is vital for our health to discover and regularly practice the things that make us feel good like this, because science has discovered under the microscope that the body runs more healthily when endorphins are flowing well.

It is very reassuring that science has now proven the common-sense knowledge that if you feel good it's actually good for you and for the health of your body.

Dr Dean Ornish of the USA wrote *Love and Survival*, a book that stresses the importance of love and intimacy for our health, as proven by population studies. Happy people, people who can cope well with stresses and life events, people who have someone or something to love, whether person or pet, people who feel fulfilled in what they do all LIVE LONGER. They're all healthier as well. We're not just talking coughs and colds here: these people have less cancer, less heart attacks, less strokes!

Sometimes, the extra health gain people get from love and intimacy can outweigh the ill effects of smoking and a poor diet, according to Dr Ornish. He describes one group of Italian Americans who had much lower coronary artery disease, despite smoking. (Coronary artery disease can lead to heart attacks and sudden death.) He worked out that this was because they all had large families, with children, parents and grandparents all living close by, and supporting each other.

Experiments on rabbits also give a clue to the importance of intimacy and love. Several groups of rabbits were all fed a diet high in saturated fat, calculated to give them high levels of blood cholesterol, and subsequent clogging of the arteries. One group showed consistently, and surprisingly low cholesterol levels, protective against heart disease. The researchers could not understand why this group gave different results to all the others. That is, until one day a researcher watched the rabbits being fed. There was a difference! Can you guess? The rabbits with the low cholesterol were the only ones that the technician gave a cuddle to when he fed them, petting and stroking them!

We've all heard of people whose anger gave them an angina attack – a cramp of the heart muscle caused by tight arteries that do not allow enough blood to get through. Strong emotions, negative ones, not the love ones, produce adrenaline and other neurotransmitters that constrict blood vessels. It gives a rather tragic twist to the meaning of the phrases 'You're killing me' and 'Hardening your heart'. Perhaps popular metaphor contains some deeply hidden truths?

Of course, there are other more physical reasons why arteries get narrow and they fur up. Free radicals are rogue molecules that damage any cell they touch, including the inside walls of our arteries. Eating lots of fruit and vegetables helps combat this damage, for nature provides lots of vitamins and 'phytonutrients' which mop up free radicals, prevent cell damage and help the body's repair mechanism. However, we may choose to eat or drink free radicals in excess of what our body can cope with. Trans fatty acids, found in fried food and hydrogenated oils and fats, cause damage. Chlorine is used deliberately for its free radical content to purify our water. It does this by irreparably damaging bacteria and so killing them. Unfortunately, any free radicals left can then attack our bodies, often blood vessels, liver and gut first. Experiments on chickens by Dr J M Price in the 1960s showed that the ones which drank chlorinated water developed diseased arteries, whilst those without didn't. Hmm. Food for thought.

Let us return to endorphins for a while. It seems that doing what you really enjoy, what makes you feel really good, ensures a healthy flow of health-giving endorphins through your body. You can feel this by noticing a warm pleasurable feeling somewhere in your body. Even thinking about, or imagining something that makes you feel good, has the same effect. What are things that make you feel good, feel comfortable, feel relaxed, feel pleasure?

Please take a few moments to think about one of your favourite things to make you feel good. Notice how you feel. Enjoy the feeling. You might like to close your eyes for a few moments and allow yourself to wallow in this pleasant feeling, the Fields of Bliss as William Bloom puts it in *The Endorphin Effect*.

Just pause, relax, notice and feel pleasure.

Thank you! Do come back and join me again. Perhaps you might like to stretch your fingers or wiggle your toes to bring you back to the here and now. You have just noticed your self – you have become conscious of your energy!

If you haven't already read William Bloom's *The Endorphin Effect*, may I recommend it? He makes several key points, the first of which is:

A pleasurable event or thought
Physically triggers the production of feel-good
endorphins and brings relaxation
And
Energetically 'melts' body tension so that
benevolent wave fields can be felt and absorbed

He also says 'For health and connection, you need to trigger endorphin flow and melt your bioenergetic armour. This can be achieved by experiencing pleasure. Do what you love to do. Work with what gives you pleasure.'

By bioenergetic armour, he means the patterns of imbalance that we can lapse into, the frozen patterns of past imbalance that are locked in our Shadow, and the Denial mechanism we all use at times.

CAUSE AND EFFECT

Let's take a look back at the history of cause and effect in health. Looking at where we have come from can help us understand how mainstream thinking is evolving.

The Western Scientific Tradition started in the Renaissance. The philosopher Descartes posited an artificial split between mind and body. Essentially the doctors got the body, the church kept the soul! Until then, there had been no split, but this divide, echoed throughout Western philosophy and scientific tradition, ensured that rationalist reductionist thinking would dominate scientific and technological advance. All well and good whilst science and technology kept delivering the goods, with new advances, better living standards, and so on. And huge advances there have been. Yet many people have a deep unease that we are somehow off course, that we may be losing the plot, and that there is a whole invisible dimension to be aware of.

Newton's celebrated theory of gravity established cause and effect as mainstream thinking in the eighteenth century. Every action had its opposite reaction, and the world could be explained as a sort of machine, where each cog fitted neatly together to make a clock which ran smoothly. Einstein's Theory of Relativity hadn't been dreamt of, so nobody had any concept that matter and energy are actually interchangeable. Against this backdrop of the certainty of physical matter, and of cause and effect, developed the thinking of Louis Pasteur.

In the nineteenth century Pasteur's germ theory held sway. This stated that many illnesses, particularly infectious ones, were the direct result of outside agents such as bacteria or viruses afflicting the body. This was a very Newtonian cause and effect model, and has led to many exciting advances, such as the development of 'magic bullet' antibiotics that kill bacteria and thus alleviate illness.

Less well known was Claude Bernard, Pasteur's contemporary and rival. Bernard concentrated on the 'Milieu Interieur', the inner state of balance that the body always seeks to maintain. It is from disturbance of this Inner Balance, from disharmony, that imbalance can occur, and disease manifest. If Pasteur was concentrating solely on the seed, then Bernard emphasised the state of health of the soil. Of course, both are important – on his deathbed Louis Pasteur said 'Bernard was right, it is the soil as well as the seed'.

If our bodies are in a healthy state, there is a constant hum and flow of neurotransmitters around the body, whilst in unhealthy or diseased states there is stagnation and blockage of flow. Where have we heard about flow and blockage before?

MODERN PHYSICS

Another strand of Western science has been physics, which has moved ahead of biomedical and other sciences in understanding the nature of matter. We now understand that solid matter is really an illusion, a convenient model, for in reality, everything is composed of vibration. Atoms, once thought to be the smallest indivisible particle in the universe, are found to be nearly all empty space. Even electrons and smaller particles are in reality just probabilities as to where they really are at any one point in time. We, that is, our bodies, our emotions and our minds, are nothing but coherent fields of wave-forms.

Added to which we now have experiments that show that the spin, or harmonious balance, of a particle measured in one continent can be instantaneously influenced by the change in spin of a particle being measured in a science lab in another continent. Further experiments show that the behaviour of minute sub-atomic particles is actually influenced by what the observer expects!

Waveforms, it seems, permeate the universe, and are the template on which, for the sake of argument, matter is formed. Or rather, waveforms actually are the universe, and all its component parts – which of course includes this page, this book, the chair you're sitting on, and you and me. And the words that you are reading are causing a thought-form in your consciousness – which is also a vibration or waveform.

Let's get this quite clear, for modern physics has quietly shattered many of the assumptions upon which you and I base our lives. The whole cosmos is composed of waveforms and vibrations. Of course, we can't perceive them all with our senses, or even measure all of them with scientific instruments. But these waveforms or vibes permeate every aspect of creation. So, at a very human level, looking only at our own Earth, every vibe from earth is permeating every place and person at all times. And our thoughts and our emotions are vibes, pure and simple, as are radio waves.

What are the implications of that for you and me?

Well, it means that through you, and me, at this very moment is flowing Radio One, Radio Two, Radio Three and so on. If you want to prove this to yourself, just stand near a radio tuned to FM – you'll find the reception alter depending on where you stand. The only reason you can't hear it in your head is because you're not tuned in. However, it still means that the waves are going through you! It also means that every single radio programme, every single TV programme, and every single mobile phone conversation is going through all of us all of the time. Strange, but it's true. YUK! – when you think about the content of most of what's transmitted!

And vibes can also be created by intention, by our thought patterns. Certainly the physical manifestation of our thoughts is an easy concept to grasp, but our thoughts act even without having to have physical results. It is an old saying that Energy Follows Thought. So your thoughts, and my thoughts, are radiating out from us at this very moment, either generally, or specifically targeted, if we are thinking of someone else. We are each radio transmitters, sometimes with specific targets. So do be careful what you are thinking – and who you are sending your thoughts to!

A very important corollary is that whatever we concentrate on, we give energy to, and in giving energy, we give life force. So if we are afraid of something, we are actually giving it energy. What we resist, persists! So if we wish something to happen, the challenge is positively to expect it. If instead we fear a painful event, we actually attract it to us by giving it energy! In other words, 'Upstairs' doesn't hear the 'not' in 'I don't want x to happen' – it interprets it as 'I want x to happen'.

Please think about this idea for a moment – it affects so much of our lives on an everyday basis!

Whatever you give positive energy to, grows. If you send loving thoughts to something, it will do well. And what you resist, persists. So sort out the unresolved issues, they'll only hang around and wait for you whilst you put them off!

EASTERN THINKING ON MIND AND BODY

We've looked at how Western Science is beginning to understand energy concepts as related to health.

Yet compared to Eastern philosophies, Western orthodox science has until now largely neglected the larger issue of why a human being is, and issues of consciousness. This split, largely a split in scientific terms of mind apart from body, stems from the growth of science in the Middle Ages and the influence of Descartes. Essentially, science and medicine got the body, as long as they left the soul – and therefore consciousness – to the Church. Now, in the twenty-first century, we have the opportunity to dissolve the artificial split of mind from body.

To do this quickly and easily, we can look to Eastern philosophies to help us. The East never considered the mind and body as separate – if anything, some traditions tended to look down on the physical body as inferior. The East, that is Chinese Cosmology and Indian Ayurvedic Tradition provide well-constructed models of the relation of man to the universe and of the meaning of existence. They also give us valuable concepts of energy and its flow around the body, through the meridian system (acupuncture), and the chakras (Ayurvedic Tradition). Other tribal traditions such as the Hunas in Polynesia also have well-ordered models to explain mind-body-spirit systems.

In Chinese tradition, there is a force permeating everything in life. This force or energy is called Chi. Chi exists in the landscape, in plants, animals, and human beings. Moreover, this Chi flows around a human body in a precise fashion, conducted by meridians, invisible circuitry in the body. The harmonious flow of this Chi contributes to health, whilst stagnation and blockage can lead to ill health and physical disease.

In addition, there are two polarities to every aspect of the cosmos, including the flow of Chi. These are yin and yang, different attributes that anything can possess. Yang attributes tend to be hotter, dryer, more male, sharp and penetrating, whereas yin attributes are cooler, moister, female, soft and receptive. It gets more complicated because something yang can actually be yin compared to a greater yang! Anyway, suffice to say, in a situation there can be yin excess or deficiency, yang excess or deficiency, or, ideal for balance, a balanced quantity of yin and yang.

And, as the yin-yang symbol depicts, yin is ever begetting yang, and yang begets yin, parts of the circle of harmonious balance in life.

The Chinese tradition also considers the eternal flow of events and circumstances as being governed by cosmic forces – an area covered in detail by the *I Ching*. The *I Ching* is a book of wisdom, which can be used as guidance for human affairs and can give great insight into the greater forces at work in one's own life, or in any situation. Nothing is thought to be permanent, all is change. A wise man, it is said, will use wisdom, and be guided by the *I Ching* to make the best of all circumstances, whether favourable or not.

Ancient traditions also talk of the body having an aura or electromagnetic field around it. This field is visible to clairvoyants and others, and can be photographed using techniques such as Kirlian Photography. Stuart Wilde in *Sixth Sense* talks about there just being a physical body and an etheric, whilst some traditions talk about a physical, an etheric, an astral or emotional body, a mental body and a spiritual body. Jane Thurnell-Read, author of *Geopathic Stress*, says that the emotional body is the centre for emotions and feelings and the atmosphere around people is generated here. The mental body is the source of thought, both everyday and imaginative, whilst the spiritual body contains the sense of – and presumably connection with – the divine, and of course inspiration comes from here.

It is actually the aura that creates the physical body, acting as a template, just as information held on a computer microchip can end up transformed into the print you are now reading. In the same way, it is the transmission from the studio that dictates what comes out of the radio, however cleverly we understand the workings of the radio itself. Our bodies are the final manifestation of an energy field template, just as a flower, plant or tree is in nature. Imbalances in the energy field later manifest themselves as physical illness. Blockages in the energy field create disease – so to be healthy, it makes sense to work at healing the energy field.

Some diagrams of the human energy field show the various bodies surrounding each other like a wooden Russian doll, but in fact just as we are penetrated by radiation and TV frequencies, the frequencies of each of these bodies permeates each other. It's probably just simpler, as Stuart Wilde says in *Sixth Sense*, to think of the physical and the 'other one' – etheric, he calls it. You and I may not be able to see it as many clairvoyants can, either as a cocoon of light around us, or in more detail with colours and swirls of energies – but we can certainly feel it. In fact there's a simple exercise we could run through to show how energy exists (most people can make this one work, and children seem always to be able to!)

Just sit back a minute and slowly bring your hands together, out in front of you, palm to palm. Allow your awareness to concentrate on your palms. As your hands become closer, you may well feel a resistance between them at a certain point – this is your energy field. Not surprisingly it feels sort of bouncy, not solid. As you move your palms through this the feeling goes. If you felt nothing, just try again starting with your hands a metre apart. Now, let's repeat that exercise, but first, let's energise the system. Please rub your hands together briskly for a few moments. Now, slowly bring them together again, from a metre apart. Feel anything? Different to last time? For most people, rubbing their hands will raise one's energy level there, and you will feel the resistance at a greater distance than the first time we did it. Don't worry it you didn't feel anything, there may be other factors at play.

Subtle energy theory also permeates the Indian tradition of Ayurvedic Medicine. This tradition talks about the three doshas – vata, pitta and kapha – as forces to be balanced within man (and woman). Methods used include diet, yoga, exercise, etc. On the subtle level, chakras exist. 'Chakra' is the Sanskrit for wheel and chakras are spinning vortices of energy. In fact they act as transformers of spiritual energy down, perhaps through the meridian/electrical system, to the more physical body, to be utilised by the nervous system.

There are seven main chakras in line with the spinal column, base, sacral, solar plexus, heart, throat, brow and crown. Each has different functions and attributes. There are also several hundred minor chakras, together with important ones in hands, feet, higher heart and others. Vital, but often not mentioned, is the fact that there are chakras above the crown, connecting to higher aspect of divine consciousness, and, most important of all for our lifetime, one below our feet, the Earth Star. This one connects with whole of our being into Mother Earth, as spiritual beings manifesting in matter. Chakras can be working harmoniously or can carry imbalances as well as being too closed or too open.

Chinese tradition sees the energy flow around the body as occurring in meridians, or energy channels. The main flow is from the crown of the head, down the centre of the back, to the sacrum, around to the perineum, and up the front of the body back to the crown. There are twelve main meridians in the body. Blockages can occur at any point on the meridians, as can low energy states. Acupuncture is the art of healing the body by working on certain points of it to release blockages, and 'harmonise' energy flows. Acupuncture uses needles to do this, whilst acupressure is the art of touching these points, also allowing healing to happen.

It seems that high-level spiritual energy is stepped down through the chakra and meridian systems into the physical body, and grounded onto the earth plane by our existence and activities. It's a bit like a 440kV high-tension cable from the power station, needing to be transformed down to 33kV, then mains 240V, and finally used to energise some rechargeable batteries. These batteries can then be used to generate the minute currents needed in computer chips. Too much energy all at once can burn us out or blow lots of fuses! On the other hand, blockages to the power supply can mean that nothing works at all, or at best ineffectively.

Our subtle energy field contains a lot of information that governs our physical bodies. This information contains all that to help our consciousness, and its vehicle, our body, to function well. It also contains all our experiences, thoughts, emotions and belief systems. It includes all our experiences and the belief systems we have absorbed through this lifetime, and also those from other times and other spaces.

Now, I'm not going to be piggy-in-the-middle over the reincarnation issue. Two-thirds of the world believes in it, one third seems not to. However, personal experience and other people's stories point to the fact that in each lifetime we are probably part of a stream of consciousness. This stream of consciousness may or may not inhabit successive physical vehicles. However, if we only get one bite of the cherry, so to speak, how do you explain someone like Mozart, who was writing concerti for orchestras at such an early age? And why do some people have very strong and personal senses of *déjà vu* in certain places, some pleasurable, some painful? Such as a friend, who feels very drawn to, and very attached to a Second World War airfield some miles away? And another friend, fascinated by transportation of convicts to Australia, who found an inscribed name on a stone which gave her a chilling sense of familiarity? And another friend, a seafarer, who on the first time he visited a certain French port, was convinced that he had sailed the same waters, only in Napoleonic times?

It's difficult to imagine that we've all had lots of lives – and there are too many people around who think they were King James, Queen Anne, Cleopatra or Caesar for everyone to have been! On the other hand, it seems that we each may be part of a greater stream of consciousness that can gather experiences and skills, and unresolved issues from other times and other places – and possibly other lifetimes. It does this as part of the learning plan that we have chosen for this lifetime.

As Above, So Below

Central to Chinese and Indian thinking is the great law of 'As Above, So Below'. Applied to subtle energies, this means that subtle energy imbalances may sooner or later manifest in the emotional and physical bodies as problems, imbalances, and possibly disease states.

Curiously, the 'As Above, So Below' esoteric doctrine very much echoes the Western Christian phrase 'On Earth, as it is in Heaven' in the Lord's Prayer. And perhaps the different vibratory frequency rates of the various invisible subtle bodies, chakras and meridians are what Jesus referred to when he said 'In my Father's house are many mansions'.

From other tribal traditions – let alone from our own lives – we learn the power of focussed thought and intention, thus proving another cosmic law – Energy Follows Thought. Mystery teachings from all ages tell us that energy follows thought. We are indeed Conscious Energy.

And the thought doesn't have to be here and now. We can draw events to us by focusing on them – although we often dismiss this as coincidence. How often have we thought, I must phone so and so – only to have them ring us, or send us a letter, or even turn up at the door!

It's modern physics that can cleverly tie all this together. Experiments have shown the effects of thought and intention on plants, even miles away. Lynne McTaggart's *The Field* elegantly puts all the research together to explain the field (or web) of consciousness that connects us all.

THE WEB OF CONSCIOUSNESS

Modern physics postulates a web of consciousness that connects us all, which we can both access for information and to imprint our own intentions. And an intention imprinted strongly enough can become fact. This applies to every aspect of our lives, positive as well as negative, so it's well worth choosing our thoughts wisely, and choosing our words even more carefully, lest we cause a mischief.

Accessing the web for information is something we can all do – a bit like browsing the World Wide Web on our computer. It happens almost automatically in daydreams, or in our sleeping dreams. A friend who is more than averagely sensitive dreamt on two nights running of an aircraft hitting a tall tower a week or so before the events of 11 September 2001.

In fact, we all have, as part of our toolkits as human beings, the ability to access the web. Clairvoyants develop this ability, the Americans and Russians both used the talent for military purposes ('Remote Viewing' 'Psychic Ops') but anyone who has ever had *déjà vu* has the talent not far below the surface.

The trouble is, in a culture where these skills are not prized, sometimes the only things that come through are either the intensely personal or the very frightening. Some years ago, I attended a dinner party. The evening was filled with humour. After the jokes wound down, one of the women present (let's call her Sarah) told about how she had nearly drowned as a teenager. As her body was saved and given the kiss of life, Sarah's consciousness had watched from above. Subsequently she became more sensitive to many things, but mentioned two in particular. One day, Sarah *knew* very strongly that her father-in-law must not travel on a specific flight to Turkey – one that subsequently crashed. On another occasion, commuting into Central London, Sarah was about to board the train in front of her, when she suddenly *knew* she must not board that train. The train ended up crashed at Moorgate Station a little while later. Gifts of intuition like this can be alarming to the person who possesses them, unless understood and harnessed. Otherwise one may feel in some way attached, responsible even, for something completely out of your control. Sometimes you just get odd feelings – unexplained, and experienced again and again, these can develop into a pile of raw unresolved fears that can bring on a panic attack.

Perhaps intuition is not a personal skill, perhaps we each have a guardian angel looking after us, but whatever the mechanism, it's probably worth 'going with the flow' rather than ignoring the subtle messages from 'the Web of Consciousness'.

The Web contains all sorts of unfiltered emotions, especially the lower astral plane, so it's vital to maintain your personal emotional balance as well, and looking at the physics of it, our vibrational integrity.

Energy follows thought, as we have seen, so it is worth working at the level of thought to heal ourselves, as ancient traditions discovered thousands of years ago.

Vibrational Medicine is the phrase used by Dr Richard Gerber which covers the area of Mind Body Spirit medicine, and includes the theories of subtle energies and therapies used to heal. These therapies include healing, homeopathy, acupuncture, flower essences, radionics (distant healing using specific tuned frequencies), the effect of colour and of course encompasses Feng Shui, the Chinese art of working with energies of the environment. Pathology also includes harmful vibrations such as those of geopathic and electropathic stress, and negative energies attached to places.

Geopathic stress is imbalance caused in us by disharmony in the earth's magnetic field. It can occur when we sleep over an energy line, which may be related to natural earth energy, or through man-made electrical fields transmitted along water lines. Electropathic stress encompasses the whole area of how our bodies (physical and etheric) are affected by electrical and magnetic fields. These fields permeate much of the world we live, work and sleep in, and are nearly always a cause of disharmony to the body. And, as we shall see in the next chapter, every threat to the body stimulates the alarm mechanism.

Nature, on the other hand, possesses much that is harmonious. Much, if not all, of nature, is built on precise geometrical harmonics, whether the scale be that of a tiny flower or that of a vast landscape. In the case of the wind causing ripples on a field of grass, or waves on the sea, we can see the waveforms of harmony. In the case of the flower or the landscape the harmony is still present, it is just less obvious. This is what we may call beauty, an uplifting waveform from nature!

So, there are environmental good vibes – and bad vibes – and also personal good vibes and bad vibes.

We each have responsibility (the ability to respond) in our lives, so it's up to us to go for the good vibes rather than the bad, and to gain full value from our journey.

Let's just repeat that:

Responsibility = Ability to choose your Response

Perhaps the aim is to achieve acceptance of the balance between good and bad, light and dark, yin and yang, and our thoughts towards ourselves – and others – can be good and loving or can withhold love.

They say it's easier to smile than to frown – it takes less muscles – and perhaps allowing ourselves to smile, to live, is to allow love to flow through us. And it seems as though love – or at least harmony and order – is the carrier wave of the flow of the universe, of the Universal flow, except when blockages get in the way.

Whether you use your intuitive gifts for personal gain or for 'the highest good of all' (a way of saying you're in Universal Flow) it's impossible to buck the flow of what must be for long. Please allow me one more personal story – and I will let you be the judge of it.

Dowsing is a way of harnessing your intuitive faculties so that you can get answers to questions. At one level, our consciousness can tap into the Web and know the answers. Some answers make us feel more comfortable and relaxed (a Yes usually does this) others (e.g. a No) make us feel tense and uncomfortable. These differences in muscle tension can be translated into different movements of a pendulum, an external indication of inner tension or a kinesiology test of finger tension. (Some people do not need to dowse, they just know the answer!)

Dowsing with a pendulum or rods, or any other way of checking your body's responses such as kinesiology, is a useful tool to access our invisible subconscious. Using a tool like this bypasses our critical faculties and can access answers hidden within. However, we can only dowse effectively if we leave personal bias out of the equation.

Dowsing can only yield helpful results when used for the 'highest good' of all concerned – something I should have remembered when I tried to dowse for the winners of some horse races. On the first I dowsed and staked £1 each way on my selected horse (£1 each way is a very timid bet!). The horses ran and I lost my pound. In the second race I chose two horses and bet £1 each way. Both lost. In the third race I bet on three horses, £1 each way on each. All three lost. On the fourth race I chose four horses, again I bet £1 each way and paid with a £20 note. Now I think I was being set up for a lesson because of what happened next. The bookmaker took £1 each way on three horses and £10 to win on an outsider. The protest I was about to make about his mistake died in my throat as I heard a little voice saying 'Andrew, just wait and see what happens'. I held my breath, and waited. The next minutes passed ever so slowly. And what happened? My outsider won at odds of 10 to 1, yielding one hundred pounds. The first decent win I've had on the horses so far, I hasten to add! Of course, in my enthusiasm I bet in the next two races – and lost each time, despite messages that told me to stop. In my eagerness I failed to notice the messages. The first was a mistake that I noticed that I pointed out to the bookie – the message was 'Andrew, you're making a mistake'. The second was when I was about to place my second bet and noticed a patient of mine who had a bad back – the hint was 'Back off!'. So I lost some of my winnings. And the lesson for me – 'Things can only happen when they're meant to happen in the greater scheme of things.' Not a bad way to be given the lesson that really in life our talents are meant to be used for the highest good of all, not just for personal gain. In other words, in life it's worth staying in balance, staying grounded, and accepting the flow of lessons as part of the journey of life.

WORDS

There's one final area to look at before leaving 'Conscious Energy'. This is the concept of words – the words we choose.

Babies communicate and without using words. So do animals. So do we all, in many non-verbal ways. Words are useful tools to solidify concepts and thoughts, and to pass information on to someone else. We tend to use words with such frequency and familiarity, and allow them to surround us in papers, magazines, books, radio and messages, that we take them for granted.

However, the energy that words convey can have tremendous importance. They have power when used as commands, to express will – and they have power in conveying information. They have power in expressing – and evoking – emotions.

Words can act as blessings or as curses. If you think this sounds a little over the top, listen carefully to the next few conversations you have, and ask yourself 'Which are the blessings, and which the curses that I am uttering?' You may be surprised – even simple statements such as 'Over my dead body', 'Don't you dare do that (or I'll. . .)', 'Blow you', and many more offensive ones are commonplace everyday curses – though not thought of as such.

Often forgotten is the importance that they have to the person uttering them. How often have we heard someone say something, and thought 'You ought to listen to that yourself!' And how often have we said something, then suddenly realised that really we are speaking to ourselves! I don't mean that the other person has walked off, but that we suddenly realise that we are talking for our own benefit, that we are articulating thoughts and feelings for us to listen to ourselves.

Actually, if we listen carefully to what we say in life, there are many messages that we vocalise meant as much, if not more, for ourselves as for the other person. It is as if the conversation between the two people is a process of each allowing themselves to bring out thoughts from within, make these thoughts firmer, more solid, more anchored in reality, and for each to become more aware of these thoughts, articulated and given substance as words.

If we can bear to listen, both to others, and to ourselves, words can give us great insight into where the next piece in the jigsaw of life should fit.

So, on our journey of experience as Conscious Energy, words can often act as clues and pointers.

In *Work and Worth*, Tony Humphreys says the two important areas we can go out of balance is in loving our self, or ourselves, and in losing our enthusiasm for learning in life. If we see ourselves, our bodies, as vehicles for an aspect of the Web, the universal consciousness, then it's worth looking after our vehicle (our body) and enjoying the journey – loving ourselves and keeping up our enthusiasm for the journey. Keeping a healthy body isn't easy – let's look at some of the physical factors that can influence our emotional health.

CHAPTER 4

Physical Influences on our Emotional Well-Being

In a book on unlocking our emotions, I should perhaps apologise for a chapter on our physical bodies. However, there are lots of physical factors that affect the way we feel, so let's look at some of them.

Our physical bodies have developed over millions of years of evolution. This evolutionary process is thought to have started with a chemical soup, developed through single cells, and ended up with bodies similar to those of higher animals, such as monkeys and chimpanzees. The route may well have come via an evolutionary chain of tiny animals, fish, and various mammalian forms. Coded information for the development of a body is stored within our DNA.

Our physical bodies are the vehicles for our consciousness, they are the cars that take us on the journey of life. As such, it's well worth our while learning what makes them tick and how to keep them working well. Otherwise, the car gets tired/old/runs out of fuel/its engine seizes up etc., and the journey stops or at least is disrupted. Actually, it's quite curious in life how your car can reflect your health. A while back, my windscreen cracked, a wing mirror broke, and the driver's door handle snapped. All at a time when my vision for my life had been let slip. I wasn't fully looking either at where I was going or at what I was leaving behind me, and my grip on life's direction had weakened. Complete coincidence of course! (Coincidence, as they say, is God's way of remaining anonymous.) Many counsellors advise that if you want to see how your life is going, look at your car, your computer and the other things you use regularly!

How our consciousness gets into our bodies is a moot point. Scientific evolutionary theory from Darwin onwards would suggest that we just happen to have evolved consciousness. Many religions, on the other hand, have a creation myth integral to their philosophy. This creation myth varies, but essentially involved a 'Fall of Man', which could be the entering of Higher Consciousness into a physical vehicle. Take your pick between Darwin and the Creation myth, it probably doesn't matter how we got here as much as what we're doing now!

Animals have only two basic urges – survival and reproduction. If you don't survive, that's it for you. And if you, or someone else in the species doesn't reproduce, then that's it for the species.

Being humans, within an animal body, we naturally have both these urges deeply embedded in our consciousness. Reproduction is a basic biological urge we all have, either very obvious, or deeply buried. Young adult animals (and humans) often have these urges close to the surface, almost ready for any opportunity. However human society has rationalised sexual behaviour to a greater or lesser extent in order to enable families to happen. Nevertheless, our biological urges are still there and can play havoc with our lives on occasions, if inappropriately expressed.

We need to survive, we have a deep need within our animal ancestry that drives us to survive, to fight our way out of a situation or to fly away from it. And to catch our prey, to find, trap and kill in order to eat, or to kill another creature or species that threatens us. We suspect that animals do all this instinctively, so a lion killing a wildebeest is not murdering it with malice, it is just acting out it's natural instincts in order to feed. Animals have a 'fight or flight mechanism' – the sympathetic nervous system in the body, mediated by adrenaline. Some animals mainly fight (and sometimes kill) other animals, others mainly flee. Should the situation demand it, the fighter can flee or the flyer fight.

Horse Sense for People by Monty Roberts is a book full of insights into the behaviour of the horse and how people can learn lessons from this beautiful animal. In essence a peaceful grazing creature, the horse is the ultimate flight animal, running from danger at high speed. In nature, horses are gregarious, living in large groups for mutual protection and nurture. Any lone horse in a plain can be easily picked off by a predator. However, given a situation when it is cornered, a horse will become a vicious fighter, using its hooves to kill an enemy.

A lion on the other hand spends much time resting and some time hunting. The fast and furious part of the hunt will only be a small portion of the final chase and kill.

What is this mechanism in the animal that enables it to fly or fight?

The nervous system of the body is in two parts. One part is the central nervous system which regulates movement, sensation, speech, vision and so on. The other part, relevant to us here, is the autonomic nervous system. Of course the two are interlinked, but it is the autonomic nervous system that regulates the body's functions, such as digestion.

The autonomic nervous system is itself in two parts, the sympathetic and the parasympathetic nervous systems. The sympathetic is the fight or flight mechanism, the para-sympathetic more concerned with digestion, reproductive function, and longer term maintenance. To digest effectively, we need to be relaxed and comfortable – the parasympathetic can crudely be thought of as the relaxation mechanism.

The sympathetic however, comes into action whenever there is a threat to survival. 'Alert, alert' messages go out, blood flow to the heart and muscles increases ready for flight. Blood flow to functions not immediately essential for survival is shut down, such as the digestive organs. Messages in the sympathetic nervous system also travel to the adrenal glands, which are next to the kidneys. Adrenaline is poured out causing changes in blood flow by opening up some arteries and constricting others. So if you exercise or swim soon after a meal, you're more likely to get cramp – or at least indigestion – as the blood supply that aids digestion becomes constricted, so that the body can change into alert mode.

The result of the adrenaline in the bloodstream is for us to feel more alert, highly sensitive to surroundings, somewhat anxious (if not actually dead scared!) with dry mouth, sweaty hands, heart pounding, and breathing more deeply. The feeling the body has is either to fight or to run away – and for humans it may be either, but often it is to run away. If you don't, your blood pressure rises for a while.

Of course, if we then use this mechanism to do some exercise, running, cycling, swimming or any other physical sport, the benefits are two-fold. The first is the release of endorphins which give us a good feeling. The second is the beneficial effects of exercise on our general level of health.

If you've ever experienced a panic attack, you will recognise the picture I've just described – a body and mind keyed up, ready to run away, caused by the effects of adrenaline. At the same time as they release adrenaline, the adrenals also pour out cortisol, as we saw in the last chapter. Cortisol is part of the natural repair and regulation system of the body. We need cortisol, but too much on a regular basis can handicap the repair mechanisms in the body.

In other words, long-term over-stimulation of the adrenals by the sympathetic nervous system can cause us various problems, some of which affect the health of the body, but some of which can directly affect our emotions and feelings.

Now, animals don't drink tea, coffee or cola, but there are substances in beverages called xanthines (caffeine is one). These xanthines alert the body like adrenaline giving a buzz. And too much can cause physical symptoms. In addition, if we eat refined sugar, the body quickly absorbs it, blood glucose levels rise sharply, much more sharply than if we eat complex carbohydrates such as rice, bread and potatoes. The pancreas releases insulin to compensate. The result of this is to reduce blood sugar too sharply, as there has been a excessive surge in supply. The body interprets this as a threat, and starts secreting adrenaline. It is possible for us to become used to adrenaline on a regular basis, and even become addicted to the buzz it may give – but there's a downside.

Ted was fifty. He complained to me of feeling anxious, having a pounding heart (sometimes irregularly), sweating hands, and heavy breathing. Talking to him, I found out that he drank ten mugs of strong coffee and tea a day, all with sugar. (Refined sugar causes an upset of the body's sugar-regulating mechanism, mediated by the pancreas. The resulting insulin surges can themselves cause adrenaline to be released). Ted was starting to develop anxiety symptoms. By changing what he drank he changed how he felt, once he had come off the buzz of the tea and coffee. In fact, Ted had been addicted to these stimulants and craved them. First thing he did every morning was to have a cup of tea.

We can see that fight and flight is the body's response to a threat, or to stress. Curiously our bodies fire off this flight or fight response to any threat, whether predator, getting cold, emotional stress, starvation, or noxious (harmful) stimuli such as bad or poisonous food, or invisible harmful electromagnetic vibes, or loud shocking noises.

There are many stimuli in our everyday world, and each is capable of evoking the fight or flight response. Our bodies have developed the phenomenon of Tolerance, or Adaptation, to help us cope, but this may cause problems in the medium and long term, as Prof. Hans Selye showed in his General Adaptation to Stress Theory.

In the 1930s Selye did some classic experiments on rats. He took two groups. One group were 'happy rats' – well-fed (not overfed), warm (not too hot) and comfortable. They scampered around their cages (one presumes) and lived happily on and on and on. They were not stressed for survival and presumably satisfied their other biological urges. Alas, the literature does not tell us these finer details, but we may presume that they were fulfilled. The second group of rats was located identically in every way – except in respect of temperature. The outside temperature was chilled to 4°C. This group of rats showed very interesting behaviour which Selye called the Adaptation Syndrome. The first phase (when cold was first applied) was Alarm. The rats were upset and no doubt shivered. After a short alarm phase, Tolerance developed, and the rats appeared outwardly normal. If at some point the cold stimulus was withdrawn, a short phase of return to normal would be characterised by a small rerun of the first alarm phase (shivering, upset). However, if the cold continued, despite looking externally normal, the rats died off long before their expected lifetime, as measured by the first group, the ones who had not been chilled. They suffered 'Terminal Decompensation'

Just to repeat, the reactions to a repeated stress or stresses are in turn, Alarm, Adaptation (Tolerance) and Decompensation.

Looking closely at the rats, Selye found that the Alarm Phase was characterised by a massive outpouring of adrenaline and cortisol and the adrenaline glands were shrunken. During the phase of Tolerance, the adrenal glands became hypertrophied and overgrown in order to cope. In the Terminal Decompensation, the adrenals became exhausted and shrivelled up. Importantly for you and I, Selye found that whatever the stimulus or stress, the rat body (and so the human) will react to a noxious stimulus with this fight or flight mechanism, and then the Alarm, Adaptation, and Tolerance sequence will set in.

Once you are tolerant to something, repeated minor stimuli are necessary to stop you going into a withdrawal phenomenon. This is why many people crave tea or coffee or other stimulants, and why Ted *had* to have a mug of strong tea first thing every morning. He also found if he drank none for three or four hours, such as during a long drive, he'd develop a headache – a classic withdrawal phenomenon.

Food addictions are far more common than is thought. Food intolerance is very common, though often unrecognised. However, any breast-feeding mother will gladly tell you how curry, sprouts, broccoli or baked beans upset her child!

Thank you for bearing with me on that explanation of the physiology of the sympathetic nervous system. You see, understanding how the body reacts to harmful or noxious stimuli is key to understanding how we react to our environment. This includes the air we breathe, the food we eat, the water we drink, the chemicals, colours, shapes and smells we come into contact with, and the vibes that affect us. Vibes include emotions, other peoples harmful thoughts, scenes we see on television or in our imagination, electromagnetic and geopathic stress, and other invisible energies.

Vibrant Physical Health

Vibrant physical health goes along with vibrant emotional and mental well-being. To be vibrantly healthy, we need good posture, good breathing, good physique, fresh air, sunlight, exercise, the right temperature and climate, adequate sleep, adequate stimulation (but not too much), high quality food (with appropriate mineral and vitamin balance) and clean water, a well functioning digestive system and a positive presence of healthy emotions.

We need time and space to breathe in a relaxed manner, to digest our food, to sleep, to relax, to have relationships with ourselves, other people and with nature. We need the stimulus and the positive harmonious vibrations and colours of nature. We need harmonious sound. As an aside, fascinating work has been done in Japan by Masuru Emoto on the effects of music on the vibrational content of water, stored as memory and detected by the crystal formations at freezing point – classical music such as Bach produces beautiful harmonious patterns, whilst heavy rock music produces degenerate discordant patterns. His book, *The Message from Water*, contains stunning photographs illustrating these points.

We need the right balance of nutrients in our cells, and the right balance of healthy bacteria in our intestines. We need to be free from parasites, noxious chemicals, including heavy metal residues (cadmium, mercury, lead and others), from free radical damage (rogue chemicals in food and drink that damage cells), from harmful electrical fields, and from food or other addictions, or the adaptation syndrome. We need a healthy circulation to send nutrients and oxygen to all parts of our body, and to remove waste products and carbon dioxide. We need to be free from emotional imbalances.

We need to have felt nurtured in the past, and to feel supported in the present. Our bodies many need support from herbs and nutrients. Any illness in the past can have left its stain on us, manifesting as a lessening of health and vitality.

In total, the factors that diminish our health and vitality are:

* Our past experiences and illnesses
* Lack of fresh air
* Lack of sunlight
* Lack of exercise
* Harmful climate
* Getting chilled/burnt/soaked etc
* Air quality
* Environment quality – including chemicals
* Lack of exposure to nature
* Not breathing correctly
* Poor posture
* Food and water – low quality, insufficient variety, insufficient vibrancy, insufficient minerals and vitamins
* Poor digestion, and imbalances of the bacteria in our large intestine, including candida (yeast) overgrowth
* Food intolerances
* Exposure to chemicals, radiation, geopathic and electromagnetic stress
* Heavy metals
* Lack of herbal and other support
* Lack of energy balance (chakras, meridians, subtle bodies)
* Unresolved emotional issues
* Illnesses in the family line (e.g. a mother who had TB) which can show as a stain in homeopathic terms

There are many good sources of information on these factors, so please forgive me if I limit our discussion to some generalisations and a few illustrations taken from real life.

Naturally, to be healthy we need to concentrate on the positive and eliminate the negative! So it's worth us all learning about posture, breathing, nutrition, food and chemical intolerance, and all the other factors noted above (plus the ones we haven't discussed – see if you can work out which ones they are!)

Breathing in a calm and connected way, slowly in through the nose, and out again, tongue behind the upper teeth, is a powerful way of reconnecting and rebalancing ourselves. Try speeding up your breathing, and notice how your emotions change. Now slow down, and notice the calming effect. The depth of breath also matters. Many of us only breathe into our upper chest, forgetting to use our diaphragm to expand both chest and abdomen. Breathing abdominally uses our whole lung capacity more effectively, and helps us function better. Interestingly, at a time of emotional imbalance, we often forget to breathe properly, instead catching our breath, or using shallow fast breaths – and helping to trap the unresolved emotion within us. Breathing rhythmically can restore balance – and using techniques such as Transformational Breathing can resolve trapped emotional imbalances. More about this technique in Keep Cleansing, Stay Grounded.

It was Hippocrates, the father of medicine, who said 'Let food be your medicine and medicine be your food', implying that a healthy diet was the key to physical health. Feel free to learn about foodstuffs, their health giving properties and vibrational and nutritional qualities. Your effort will be repaid with interest!

Eating fresh light food brimming with zest and natural goodness (sounds like an advert, doesn't it!) enhances our well-being. Eating, or overeating, heavily-processed refined calories, denuded of their minerals and vitamins, is likely to diminish our health.

Certain foods can upset us, even to the point of changing our mood. Some people feel depressed and irritated a day after eating chocolate. Aaron, aged twelve, was often hyperactive, with a difficult temper. His mother tracked down red colourings, artificial sweeteners and refined sugar as causing his mood changes. Later kinesiology testing helped her choose some mineral supplements, including magnesium, which made him even better.

Practices such as Tai Chi, yoga, breathing exercises, relaxation and meditation can facilitate health benefits. Health building therapies are useful. These include aromatherapy, acupuncture, homeopathy, Ayurvedic medicine, and others. Of course if you need surgery or antibiotics, then they too are entirely appropriate.

All health therapy and practice of medicine hopes to cure (healthy resolution) but sometimes has to settle for palliation. Palliation is the treatment of symptoms without tackling the cause. Sometimes the body is not strong enough to take treatment aiming at cure, as homeopaths will know, so one aims for palliation. Some philosophies of medicine distinguish carefully between cure (a healthy resolution) and palliation, whilst some philosophies are evolving from the thinking that 'Health = Absence of Symptoms'.

A healthy environment is key to the health of any individual, so let's just look in more detail at a few of the factors involved.

Chinese tradition looks carefully at many aspects, including lie of the land, placement of house, rooms, doorways, furniture and many other aspects. They include 'Dragon Lines' of energy in the earth. This art is called Feng Shui, and is now widely written about.

Electromagnetic stress is now being understood as a major hidden contributory cause of illness. Electric power is pretty new in evolutionary terms. In the second half of the twentieth century we've seen the spread of alternating current around the world giving many benefits. Radio and television broadcasting, and lately satellite and mobile phones have developed rapidly to encompass the world. Basic physics tells us that every wire carrying a current has a field around it. In addition, electric motors (such as hairdryers, hoovers, fridges, and washing machines in the home), alternators in cars and transformers, at every level from high tension cables to mains/battery radios all produce electromagnetic fields. So do televisions, computers, and so on, as do electric lights.

The world, especially our homes, is full of electromagnetic smog. What's more, water is a conductor of both electricity and magnetism. Our bodies are 70% water, and there is often water underground, below our homes. Any transformer or electric motor sends a vertical column of electromagnetic field to the earth (and vertically above itself). If this column hits a rivulet of water, the rivulet now sends up a thin field of electromagnetism throughout its length. What is more, we may sit or sleep in this field.

Our world is now filled with electromagnetic vibrations that are artificially produced. The vast majority of this extraneous electromagnetic smog is not beneficial to our health – in fact, it is positively harmful.

Now I have a problem personally. If I use a mobile phone, within half a minute I have a headache and start to slur my speech (although certain flower essences will neutralise this imbalance); whilst sitting close in front of the high power cathode-ray tube of older computers gives me a feeling of nausea and malaise within minutes. (I'm writing this on a laptop, which produces much lower levels of electromagnetic smog.) 'OK, Andrew', you may say, 'So that's you – but personally I don't have a problem.' Well, firstly I'm pleased for you – it's my problem that I may be over-sensitive in this area. However, please take note, because knowledge about this whole field is rapidly increasing. Just because you don't actually notice anything, it doesn't mean there isn't a problem – merely that you haven't noticed it! For instance, if you do have an electric blanket, please unplug it at night at least, or ideally use a hot water bottle instead, so that you avert irradiating your whole body with an electrical field. Some countries are well aware of this sort of invisible problem. In Germany, for instance, it has been long known that certain houses are at risk of 'Geopathic Stress' (as the electromagnetic field coming up from the earth is called). Such houses seem to lead to a greater incident of cancer among the occupants. However, by moving the beds and furniture, often the danger can be averted.

Some Case Studies

Electromagnetic Stress

Richard was brought in to see me by his mother. Eight-year-olds rarely get headaches, yet Richard had suffered from one for six weeks. Careful enquiry revealed a recent change around of his bedroom. On the other side of the wall from the head of his bed, a television had been placed. Simply unplugging this at night stopped his headaches, as moving it would also have done.

Chemical Intolerance

Deirdre had chronic ill health, with headaches, tiredness, weakness, and difficulty in concentrating. Blood tests showed a low thyroid, but replacement treatment did not cure her. Her job involved being exposed to many solvents in her office. A chemical intolerance was diagnosed, which didn't start to resolve until she left that job for another, thus avoiding the causative agents.

Nutritional Imbalance

Sarah was sixteen and complained of tiredness, low mood, and inability to shake off colds. She ate no fruit or vegetables and drank several soft drinks every day. Merely changing her diet to involve her drinking more water, eating fruit and vegetables, and cutting down on junk food, changed her health, vitality and personality.

Chocolate Addiction

Judy was twenty-five. She had recurrent headaches, and was again laid up in bed with abdominal pain. She'd felt unwell for months. She used to eat two large bars of chocolate most days. Stopping this cured her symptoms – but not without a withdrawal phase which lasted three days, during which she felt more ill. She was glad she stuck it out because the reward was freedom from symptoms, a clear head, and new vitality.

Adrenaline Addiction

Andrew was forty-three, and good at his job. He was also an ideas person and would enthusiastically try to implement his latest ideas. Over-tiredness due to overwork contrarily led him to try even harder. He became irritable and snappy at times. It took a family crisis for him to realise that he had been addicted to the kick of adrenaline for several years and had reached the point of exhaustion. He re-focused his energies, took his foot off the metaphorical accelerator, and found that life without adrenaline was actually gentler and more sustainable. It was also considerably more pleasing, not just for him, but also for everyone else around.

Many men (and women) are chronically addicted to adrenaline 'thrills' or overwork, without realising it. They often use stimulants like tea and coffee to keep them going – but after the phase of Tolerance/Adaptation, comes the Terminal Decompensation phase! So please take care to stay in balance!

Enjoy your day. Perhaps you might start a little routine as soon as you awaken, gently checking that your consciousness is back in line with your physical body. If any dreams seem significant or important, you may make a little note of them. Next you choose to stretch in bed, then allow yourself to arise and stand up straight. You might stretch your arms to the sky, plant your feet firmly on the ground, and allow yourself to feel connected to both heaven and earth, acting as a metaphorical bridge between the two. Some deep breaths of vibrant, fresh air connect you with Mother Nature, whilst you give thanks that another day is ready for you to experience. (After all, waking up is definitely better than the alternative!)

Next, perhaps a few minutes of silent thought for you to consider how best you can use your energies today, whilst continuing to breathe with conscious intention. Allow your awareness to quietly check through your body, to heal and repair any imbalances that have accumulated. Feel free to give thanks when the re-balancing is complete. You are now ready for a few moments of using your physical body to recharge its batteries, with some gentle flowing movements like those in T'ai Chi, or some stretches akin to Yoga.

You may now consider what to do next. Food? A bath or shower? A walk? A journey to work? Or tasks at home?

Please feel free to consciously enjoy and be aware of each detail of your day, and allow yourself to choose to watch each detail and each event as it unfolds – and do remember to look after your physical body! Have fun! And stay in balance. Take breaks to give yourself a conscious opportunity to rebalance, stop, and listen. If in doubt, fall silent and allow the still small voice from within to offer guidance. Be patient. Don't rush, don't hurry.

Enjoy your physical body!

In the next chapter, we'll look at our emotional in-tray, and all the unresolved issues that go to make up our Shadow.

CHAPTER 5

What's in My Shadow? Blots, Stains, Tangles and Cobwebs

D o you remember the Map of Emotional Healing that we looked at back in Chapter Two? Just to refresh our memories, here it is again

Life = Journey of Experiences
Experience = Event + Emotional Reaction

The Map of Emotional Resolution

Emotional Reaction

Is either

Fully experienced

Expressed and Evaluated

and finally

Resolved

to be

Integrated into life's lesson

or

Incompletely Experienced (or not at all),

Repressed, denied, buried, distracted, avoided

then

Unresolved, placed into 'Shadow' to

Await future reprocessing

The mechanism we use to keep issues unprocessed and in our Shadow:

* Denial

The means we use to stay in Denial:

* Repression
* Distraction
* Projection
* Comfort behaviour
* Risk-taking
* Escape into Fantasy
* Blotting it out
* Overwhelm

And later reprocessing

* Relive
* Relieve
* Experience
* Express
* Resolve
* Integrate

So what exactly is our Shadow?

OUR SHADOW

Our Shadow is a vital loving, accepting, non-judgmental part of our selves. It is invisible to our eyes, but sometimes we can feel it. Our Shadow carefully collects for us all our unresolved experiences, all our unfulfilled desires, and holds them carefully for us until we are ready to deal with them.

Our Shadow may also contain packages of skills ready to be accessed and used when the time is right.

When the time is right, our Shadow can surrender up to us unresolved experiences and issues for us to resolve. And as we remember, we resolve the experiences by Reliving, Relieving, Experiencing, Expressing and Resolving. The result, of course, is an Integrated Experience – lesson finally learnt, driving test passed.

We all live our lives in denial of our Shadow, to a greater or lesser degree, fearful of acknowledging it, for to acknowledge the problem is to start dealing with it. It is fear that keeps us in denial, for we find ourselves emotionally entangled with shards of Emotional Broken Glass, with issues we feel uncomfortable, silly, guilty, angry about or disgusted with. And the thought of having to deal with something now, or in the future, with something that we never resolved at the time of first experiencing fills us with fear. Fear of pain, and fear of failure.

It is fear that stops us doing what is best for us, fear that makes things too difficult or painful, and so we consign all sorts of issues into our Shadow. What happens next? We bury them deeply, or pretend that the issues don't exist. All through fear. Fear of pain, and fear of failure.

Fear is the lock. May I please repeat that. Fear is the lock. And if fear is the lock then love is the key. Loving acceptance is the catalyst that can melt fear and start to resolve buried issues from our Shadow, and thus reharmonise patterns of imbalance.

Yet if we do 'Feel the fear and do it anyway', actually it never seems so bad after all. A bit like my tax returns. I have to confess at this point that I am not a particularly tidy or methodical person. OK, I can have good ideas (sometimes), and I love communicating and chatting, sharing experiences and energy with other people, but I'm not very good at getting down to certain things. I'm not that organised or tidy. I do hope you can sympathise with me, but then what do you expect from a Gemini with Libra rising! So, my tax returns generally take me six months and three hours. Why six months and three hours, you may well ask? Well, six months of putting it off, fretting about them and worrying – six months of avoiding the issue – and three hours to actually do the paperwork and send it off! So why don't I deal with it all in the first place? My excuse is Gemini with Libra rising, I suppose – which really means that I have no good reason at all. And, I have to admit, I feel pretty good when I have finished the mere three hours work it takes to do the tax returns.

Can you see how pushing something away and avoiding it doesn't really help at all? What we resist, persists. The issue or job still has to be dealt with in the end – so we might as well get straight on with it now – or at least as soon as convenient!

So the key is Loving Acceptance. Acceptance and non-judgment of ourselves. One of the things about being human is that we learn early in life to give ourselves a hard time, to punish ourselves, to divide the world into good and evil, to judge everyone and everything, to make comparisons and judgments. In doing so we make judgments not just about other people, but also about ourselves. We learn that there are bits of ourselves that are not good – and rather than accept them, we often pretend they don't exist, or excuse them with a trivial explanation that convinces nobody, let alone ourselves. But at least we can pretend it's not there!

To keep up this pretence – that our less attractive sides don't exist – that is to say, that we have unresolved emotional business awaiting processing, stuck in the in-tray, what do we do?

Remember the map of Emotional Healing? Of course, we use Denial. And, if the issue comes dangerously close to our awareness, if it starts to surface, we use Repression, Distraction, Avoidance, Projection, Comfort behaviour, Risk-taking behaviour, Escape into Fantasy, Blotting it out, and finally, Overwhelm.

What's more, we sometimes hide some good bits of ourselves, because we desperately crave love. Love is needed for survival by all living things. We can see this from observing animals and plants, how they thrive if tended and nurtured. We say a good gardener has green fingers – we actually mean that that gardener gives a lot of love to the plants and so they grow well.

If a small animal is separated from its mother, and cut off from love and attention, it will not thrive or grow well. A period of mourning, or feeling of loss, is experienced, and the young animal may die, even if there is adequate food and water. Every farmer can vouch for this. If they look after their animals well, and care for them, then they do better than if they are neglected.

So why would we hide bits of ourselves to gain love? One of the major pressures in life is that to conform, to be acceptable to others, to meet other peoples' expectations. This is true of families, schools, companies, and every walk of life. Uncritically, we often assume that these expectations are valid, that they are fair and just, and there for our benefit! Well, a rude shock is in store for us when we examine some of these expectations and prejudices.

All the same, early in life we learn to behave in ways that gain us approval, even though these ways may not be true to our Inner Self, our own Truth. We know how to elicit a 'Good boy, good girl', and are upset by criticism that can wither and push us back into our shell. 'Bad boy, bad girl, don't do that, No, you mustn't, you can't, you shouldn't!' The 'Shoulds' and 'Shouldn'ts' of life weigh heavily on our shoulders.

The first three words many children learn are Mummy, Daddy and No. NO! Why on earth should we learn a negative, something that blocks natural flow? Because all too often, that's what we hear. So we learn to adapt, to do things that meet approval, even if this means hiding our natural abilities and talents. How many people have spent their lives, let alone their childhoods, denying aspects of their spontaneity, their creativity, because it met with disapproval – or because they felt they OUGHT to do this, or HAD to do that? Even when they knew within that it wasn't quite right – or was badly wrong?

Sometimes families coerce people into denying their truth. One of the saddest stories I have heard was that of a girl in her twenties. She finally plucked up courage to seek help to deal with the issues of childhood physical and sexual abuse, only to find that her family rejected her and ganged up on her. Why? Her grandfather had abused her. To accept this in the family, even though the man was now dead, was more than most of the members could do. So for fifteen years, this girl had been considered a liar by her mother and father, and had had to live with a painful unresolved truth. She had retreated into herself, given up music and dance, and took refuge in trying to be mediocre, to live a grey uneventful life that threatened nobody. And when she did finally take the step to stand in her own truth, and heal with unresolved emotional pain, she lost any family support she'd ever had – not that it had ever helped her over one key issue.

What then is our Shadow, our Devil side as it used to be called? (Devil is Lived spelt backwards, just as Evil is Live reversed.)

Our Shadow is part of our Self. It is that aspect of ourselves which we do not accept, that we reject. It is the sum of all our unresolved experiences – those issues that we have not yet dealt with or accepted.

Jannet Unite-Penny explains our Shadow in the following way. I am indebted to her for allowing me to quote from her forthcoming book on the South African Flower Essences.

Understanding the Shadow side of ourselves is one of the major challenges to humanity today, particularly as it holds the key to transforming ourselves and, thereby, our world. Please bear in mind that the subject of the Shadow is too vast to begin to do it real justice in a short article of this nature. Although I am also writing about how to use The South African Flower Essences in the context of working with the Shadow, I will discuss the Shadow first, in some detail, before looking at the relevant flower essences.

Many of us have heard the term 'Shadow' without really understanding what it means. Perhaps we have some vague idea that it may be a rather undesirable part of ourselves and feel that it is best ignored. Maybe we imagine it to be dark, or evil and, consequently, tend to be rather afraid of it and avoid the whole issue. Thus, the subject of the Shadow often remains a mystery, swathed in misunderstandings.

So, let's look, then, at what the Shadow is and why it is relevant to our daily lives.

It was Carl Jung who first popularised the concept of the Shadow in his work with the unconscious aspects of the self. In the *Healing Power of Illness* Dethlefsen and Dahlke define it as 'The sum of all those rejected aspects of reality which people either cannot, or will not, see within themselves and of which they are therefore unconscious.' The Shadow is actually a component of the Self, more than just the sum of its parts, and since it is always with us and holds so much of our life energy, anyone serious about increasing self-awareness or about growing spiritually, must, of necessity, tangle with this Shadow Self for the reasons we shall examine below.

A way that I, personally, find to be helpful in understanding the Shadow is as follows. When we are born, we accept our world as it is. We do not judge ourselves, the situations in which we find ourselves, or our interactions, as either right or wrong. At this stage, our sense of self could be pictured as spherical, rather like a huge beach ball, representing the totality of all that is. We do not differentiate into good or bad. We do not feel that we should not be this, or that we should be that. We just are.

Within a short time we begin to learn, in very practical ways, that this is a reality of duality. We learn that there are expectations of us already firmly in place, that certain behaviour attracts positive responses and other behaviour attracts negative responses. We learn that we are required to live up to those expectations in order to be loved, to fit into the roles in which we have been cast, with the family dynamic, with the society into which we have incarnated. As we need love in order to survive, we learn to adapt ourselves. Thus, the process of splitting off parts of ourselves commences and we begin to divide the sphere into what we accept as part of ourselves, and what we reject.

The fact is, however, that we actually encompass both polarities, the good and the bad, the light and the dark. As Kahlil Gibran put it:

> *The whole universe exists within you*
> *And everything that is within you also exists within*
>   *creation.*
> *In a single drop of water is to be found the secret of*
>   *the boundless ocean.*
> *A single manifestation of yourself contains all life's*
>   *manifestations.*

Ultimately, we have to come to an inner understanding of this. We have to deal with each aspect, even that which we have discarded, as it holds part of our energy which we need to transmute and transform. And the Shadow is here to help us.

In life we learn to identify ourselves in certain ways. For example when we say 'I am a woman, I am a mother, I am a teacher, I am kind, I am tolerant, I am capable' or, on the other hand, 'I am unkind, I am intolerant, I am bad and I am incapable' these beliefs form part of who we see ourselves being. However, all of these ways in which we identify ourselves are choices we make and each one implies, automatically, that we are rejecting from our consciousness the polarity of what we define ourselves to be. So it is that we will deny our hostility, our rage, our deceptions or our envy. Since we are, as Gibran points out, the totality of all that is, what happens, then, to all that we exclude? The nature of reality is such that banishing aspects of ourselves from our consciousness does not cause them to disappear anymore than the ostrich, hiding his head in the sand, becomes invisible because he can no longer see his foe! It truly is a major deception we foist upon ourselves.

My favourite description of the Shadow is given by Lazaris in *Working with the Shadow* (NPN Publishing Inc). For an in-depth understanding of this subject, and, in fact, of the spiritual paradigm in general, you cannot, in my opinion, do better than the Lazaris material. He says that, particularly in our youth and young adulthood, 'It is as though our arms are filled with bundles and packages, far too much for us to carry' and so we drop things. The Shadow comes along behind us and picks it all up, the garbage, as well as the treasures, and keeps them until we are ready to deal with them. He says that the Shadow is not, as many think, our enemy but our loyal friend. It 'is there to hold sacred and protect all the stuff that we are unable to deal with and unable to accept.' So the Shadow is a part of us, a being, 'who holds for us all the stuff we deny, discount, disown and pretend does not exist.'

Along with this, it also holds all that we refuse to be responsible for and also that which is too painful for us to handle at the time, all that we hide from ourselves. Thus, the Shadow serves as a faithful friend, picking up and holding for us what we discard and disown. Its function is to keep these parts of us until such time as we are ready to take them back and recognise them as integral to who we are.

As pointed out above, it is not only the so-called 'negative' aspects of the self that we disown. The Shadow also picks up the treasures we let fall. Now, why would we disown positive aspects of ourselves, you may ask? A starting point in understanding this is to remember that, as children, our primary need is to be loved in order to survive. In order to obtain this love, we will adapt to whatever is required of us, whatever it takes to fit into the required role, even if this entails giving up abilities we innately have or taking on a negative role in the family dynamic. Perhaps a sibling is the favourite, perhaps as a boy or girl we are taught that we have to be a certain way, perhaps the family needs someone to blame, someone to take on the role of black sheep. Perhaps our conditioning is that we are bad, lazy or incompetent. Perhaps, it is not acceptable to be powerful, strong, loving, intelligent, compassionate, empathetic or sensitive. In these cases, what happens is that we may well disown the light or 'good' aspect of ourselves and, this, our Shadow Self will pick up for safekeeping.

Another helpful tool in understanding the Shadow and in obtaining insights into its way of working in our lives is the astrological chart. To those unfamiliar with a chart, it may appear at first glance to be a mass of indecipherable and incomprehensible glyphs. With study, it can come to be a fascinating source of insight into our own very individual psyches.

In looking at any chart, one usually begins with the three most important factors – the position and sign of the sun at the time of birth (commonly known as sun sign and the basis of the astrological reports you will find in the press); the position and sign of the moon and, thirdly, the sign on the horizon at the time of birth which is called the Ascendant.

The Ascendant indicates how you see yourself, how you present yourself to the world, what your sense of self is. Since determining where the Ascendant is on the wheel requires accurate information as to the exact time and place of birth, the average person is often unaware of what their Ascendant is. Unfortunately, this is such an important source of information that the lack thereof results in incomplete interpretation of the chart.

Well, what does all this have to do with the Shadow? On the wheel of an astrological chart, the Ascendant marks what is called the cusp of the first house. As the wheel turns, the Ascendant moves from the horizon up into the light of awareness of self. In a diagonal line, directly across the chart, the area moving down, away from the light and into the dark, is the cusp of the seventh house which marks the Descendant. It is also the indicator of the Shadow Self. Situated as it is, in opposition to the area of which we have the most awareness, this is the part of ourselves of which we have the least consciousness, the part of ourselves we disown and consequently, tend to project outwards onto others, situations or our realities in general.

Fittingly, this Descendant marks the section of the chart that deals with our relationships with 'the significant other' in our lives, the person upon whom we are most likely to project the disowned aspects of ourselves. Initially, we are likely to fall in love with our Shadow's characteristics. The person who openly displays what we deny in ourselves has enormous attraction for us – in them we see ourselves completed. Later on in the relationship these are the very characteristics that infuriate us.

Understanding of this projection process is of crucial importance in learning how we can work with our Shadow and, thereby, reap the harvest of benefits that result from integrating it. In this process, we have set up a wonderful feedback mechanism in order to allow ourselves to attain self-knowledge which can lead us back to wholeness. Since everything we do not wish to be, or of which we do not approve, is held by the

Shadow, this is what will be mirrored to us by our outside world. In this illusion we have set up for ourselves, what we disown is presented to us in order that we may recognise it as part of ourselves. In Lazaris' words, 'When we are finally ready, the Shadow returns to us, meticulously, what it has held for us – to be processed and to be used.'

To work with our Shadow we need to look at the characteristics of the people in our lives whose behaviour pushes our buttons, at people we dislike or hate, at what irritates or angers us the most. It is very possible that we may pride ourselves on having the opposite of these particular qualities for, ironically, the more intensely we polarise ourselves in any characteristic, the more we will attract its opposite to us in our lives. Also we need to look at what we really admire in others. This is information that teaches us so much about ourselves.

The standard response we often have, when asked to look to see where we can identify ourselves in people, or in situations, which upset us or get to us in some way is 'But I don't do that!' And the answer is 'No, you probably don't but maybe you would really like to'. Perhaps what stops us is the judgment we have on such behaviour that prevents us allowing ourselves to act in such a way. It follows that we are really infuriated when someone else has the audacity to do so! Similarly, when we admire someone passionately and long to be like them, try to identify the quality in them that triggers this response and work on reclaiming it from your Shadow.

We should also look at the feedback we get in life – what do people tell us that we don't like to hear, what are we ashamed of, what do we hide (even from ourselves), what patterns do we repeat in our lives? These are important ways in which our Shadow communicates with us. With practice and perseverance, we can find, in these areas, the hidden keys to understanding the disowned aspects of ourselves which the Shadow holds in waiting for us.

So the secret is to sit by yourself, calling on your Higher Self and unseen counsellors to help you and to give yourself time to work with whatever it is that evokes this response in you or that you have identified. With real self-honesty and integrity, examine the depths of your psyche. Admit the truth to yourself. I am not suggesting you need to admit the truth to anyone else nor that you go into the adolescent part of yourself and start beating yourself up about it. Castigating yourself or going off on a blaming trip of 'Oh, I am such a despicable, horrible person, no one could possibly love me!' is going to achieve nothing at all. What is needed is the recognition of this aspect in yourself; the lifting of the judgment you have (for you judge what you disown), forgiveness of yourself – for having hidden the truth from yourself for so long – and for the pain you have caused yourself, and others, in the process and a desire to be different from now on. Then, put into practice what you have learned about yourself and actually be different.

We have a choice as to how we process the stuff in our lives, not whether we process it. We can grow through struggle and pain or through joy and adventure. Illness and crisis occur when we refuse to hear the whispers urging to us change voluntarily. The Shadow can be a very valuable teacher, if we choose to work with it.

Jannet now goes on to look at how specific flower essences can help resolve issues held by our Shadow. Flower essences, as we shall see in Keep Cleansing, Stay Grounded are powerful yet gentle tuning forks to help us resolve patterns of imbalance, and so to help us return towards patterns of harmony and balance.

So how can flower essences help us with this? The South African Flower Essences produce a wide range of essences that includes several individual ones aimed specifically at working with the Shadow Self. Additionally, many of the other essences have very pertinent uses in dealing with the issues that arise in the context of Shadow work.

Chinkerinchee Essence is the essence that brings in a resonance of integrity, so important if we are to face truthfully that which we have hidden for so long. It assists us in developing the ability to be honest with ourselves and to act with purity of motive. Coming face to face with that which we fear in ourselves takes strength of character and courage but, through doing so, we are able to transform our reality. Borage Essence can provide a valuable boost when this courage is needed. Stretlitzia Essence helps us focus and persevere, giving us clarity of purpose and the ability to hold the vision of what we want to become and create for ourselves. Disa Essence is recommended for when it all feels too much and we hit despair and hopelessness. These are major issues we are facing and we should not underestimate the power of the emotions that may be unleashed.

Cancer Bush Essence works remarkably to assist us in confronting and transforming the ugly, or dark, aspects of our own nature. Meet and integrate these demons and there is little to fear in the outside world. Among the baggage the Shadow picks up and carries for us are our hostility, our anger, pride, greed and lack of morality. These are not very pretty and facing them can cause considerable apprehension and inner torment. What we fear tends to come at us in life. The Shadow draws people, circumstances and experiences to us so that we can become whole. When we find ourselves battling in the inner world, confronting fears that are generated by the disowned parts of ourselves, Cancer Bush Essence is the one to use. It helps us transform the dark and ugly aspects of our nature. If this generates fear Coral Tree Essence is amazing for alleviating generalised feelings of fear and Cape Almond Essence is a wonderful essence for grounding, centring and providing a sense of safety and security while you process these aspects of your nature.

When we polarise ourselves in the upright, moral side of ourselves, disowning our ability to be violent or hostile, judging this behaviour in others, there is the potential to meet this violent side of ourselves out in our world. Reality manifests from the inside out. The dark, Mr Hyde, aspect of self may be represented to us by our realities, not to punish us, but to teach us to recognise these energies within ourselves and in order that we take back the power we have given away to outside forces in our lives. On a spiritual level we already know this.

Another important essence for dealing with these violent or abusive aspects, which we have projected outward, is Wild Ginger Essence. It facilitates the owning and accepting of these aspects, drawing them out of Shadow consciousness and allowing them to be transmuted. We all know, perhaps first hand, of people who find themselves, repeatedly, in abusive relationships, replaying the old patterns set, most probably in childhood. The way to deal with this is to own this pattern so that reality no longer has to keep presenting it.

Geranium Incanum Essence can also be of particular value in such destructive or vengeful relationships, where we find ourselves attracting violent, threatening situations in our lives. Consciously integrating the Shadow aspect of the self in these circumstances will free the very powerful, magnetic energy which holds us locked into such relationships. It may well be that Crisis Remedy and Auric Protection Essence could be used most beneficially here, as well.

There is the probability, in these circumstances, that you will feel victimised, failing to remember that reality is a product of the inner world. Use Yucca Essence as it works to help transform feelings of victimhood through taking personal responsibility for what happens to us.

Grevillea Essence is another essence that works to assist in the incorporation of the Shadow Self. Because judging that which we disown in ourselves, when we see it is others, is so characteristic, we may similarly feel judged and vulnerable to criticism. Understanding that we create what happens to us, that it is our judgments that are being reflected back to us, frees us to take back our power from those onto whom we have projected it and thereby change our outer realities. Pompom Tree Essence can also be used for fear of rejection, feelings of shame and vulnerability to the opinions of others and Plumbago Essence deals specifically with the feelings of shame and low self-esteem which can increase our vulnerability.

As mentioned in passing above, another major function of the Shadow is that of holding emotions for us which are too intense to deal with when we first experience them. When a loved one dies violently, when we are sexually abused, when a relationship ends, when the loss, pain, grief, abandonment or betrayal are too great or when we just cannot face the anger or shame, our Shadow will pick up these feelings and keep them until we can face them. There are many of the South African Flower Essences that are applicable in such circumstances. I will mention only a few to give you an idea of how to use them.

English Hawthorn Essence is for intense grief, when our hearts are broken, when the hurt and anguish are unbearable. We really cannot afford to leave pain of this type in our bodies, unprocessed, as it can easily lead to illness. We have to have the courage to tangle with it and this is a valuable essence to help us. Dog Rose Essence works, similarly, with unexpressed grief facilitating expression and integration of the pain. Peach Essence assists us with the effects of past trauma, or grief, which continue to effect the present. The beautiful blue Water Lily, indigenous to the Cape of Good Hope, has been used for the Water Lily Essence which benefits us when we have numbed ourselves against the pain and simply deny what we feel. Pelagonium Essence is indicated when the emotional baggage we carry results in a sense of alienation and isolation. It also facilitates the integration of the unconscious into the conscious.

In our world we are taught that anger is an unacceptable emotion – 'Nice people don't get angry!' Since we will all feel anger, regardless of whether society says we may or not, we often have to suppress it to keep it from view. Once again, the Shadow will keep this anger for us until we are ready to own it. Suppressed or depressed anger rapidly turns to poison in our lives and the sooner we deal with it, the better for us.

We can turn anger back upon ourselves to cause self-hatred and self-condemnation. It can result in depression and despair. This is when Daffodil Essence is needed. Another way that anger seeps out in our lives is when we use it passive aggressively to punish those around us, and we can be remarkably inventive in finding ways to do this. White Geranium Essence, for unreliability and irresponsibility, and Vygie Essence, for control and manipulation, are two to remember here.

Since women, in particular, are conditioned not to feel anger it is an important issue for them to bring to the surface. There are several essences that focus on this emotion in the context of female issues. The first of these, Touch-me-not Essence deals with anger that is in response to limitations and judgments imposed on women by chauvinism and patriarchy. Another is Gazania Essence for the woman who has to subjugate herself to the needs of others and who is sexually repressed. Lemon Essence is particularly helpful as an aid to processing anger in women which is disallowed by virtue of society's judgments.

The negative ego and the Shadow are very different. Whereas the former really is the enemy, seeking to destroy us at every opportunity, the Shadow, as we have discussed, is our friend. One of the negative ego's favourite games is that of superiority, feeling better (or, in some cases, worse) than everybody else. However, when we encounter pride, elitism and prejudice in our world, we may do well to look to see what messages our Shadow has for us. If prejudice and unfair discrimination make our blood boil, if we hate people who hold themselves up as being elite, above others, and if we are convinced that we would never, ever, be so arrogant, perhaps we should take Roella Essence. However much we are convinced that this is, in no way, a characteristic of ours, the intensity of our emotional response is telling us something about ourselves. Roella Essence facilitates humility and allows us perspective on ourselves.

Another way we need to seek wholeness is by incorporating our masculine and feminine sides in balance and harmony with each other. With the identification of ourselves as men or women, comes the disowning of important parts of our nature. Men will tend to disown their feminine sides and women their masculine sides, leaving it to their partners to mirror these aspects to them. Of course, we are all both and focusing on either polarity will attract situations that challenge us to change. Take a look at your interaction with the men and women in your life to gain insight into the relationship between your inner male and female. If you don't like what you see, change the inner world. The South African Inner Male Essence and Inner Female Essence Combination Essences are a valuable adjunct to growth when working with these aspects of self.

The South African Lotus Essence works on a very powerful, spiritual level to align the chakras and open the crown chakra to contact with our Higher Self, Soul and Spirit. Because so much of the resistance to growth and to attaining enlightenment is tied up in the Shadow, this essence is of great assistance in helping us integrate and incorporate our Shadow Selves. Coming into contact with the resonance of our Higher Selves breaks down the resistance to growth, allowing us to release the pain and anger of the past and transmute the energy to a higher level.

This, ultimately, is the gift of the Shadow Self – to use the discarded aspects of self it has lovingly kept for us throughout our lifetime and become whole.

(Copyright Jannet Unite-Penny – please see the Resource section for more information on the South African Flower

Essences and the Lazaris material. Do visit www.saflower-essences.com for detailed information on The South African Flower Essences with pictures and cross-references.)

Jannet has shared with us tremendous insights not only into what is in our Shadows in terms of unresolved emotions and reactions, but also described some of the most important tools to help us accept and resolve aspects of our Shadow, in flower essences, Tuning Forks from nature. Let's now try and categorise some of the things we find in our Shadow, to help us understand them, and be able to look for them.

Let's now look at What's in My Shadow?

BLOTS, STAINS, TANGLES AND COBWEBS

Inside our Shadow are many, many millions of little un-resolved issues. Some of these are personal from the present or recent past, some of them are personal from the deep past. Some of them are from our family or from tribal ways of looking at the world, and all of them are frozen patterns of imbalance that, with the correct method, can be resolved. Some of the issues are big and some are pretty small.

Some of the unresolved issues are from the deep unconsciousness of mankind, such as fears of snakes and spiders, and some are intensely personal, but from other times and other spaces. I'm not going to try and argue for or against reincarnation here – but I would suggest that we each have access to streams of consciousness that extend beyond the experiences of this lifetime. As we saw in Conscious

Energy, Mozart's incredible ability to compose at a very young age doesn't prove the issue, but I guess that either he'd been round before, or he brought in to this lifetime an amazing skills package of software ready installed onto his hard disk.

On a more personal and mundane level, my youngest daughter Rose would handle a proper book with great respect, turning pages ever so carefully, aged just one. This is an age at which most children can only be trusted with a cardboard or plastic pretend book. Where did this skills package come from? Some people say that a lot of children are wise old souls, coming in with considerable skills packages. I don't know if that is true or not, but whether we come in with just skills packages or with issues to resolve and an agenda of unresolved experiences, it can go a long way to explain certain phenomena and situations many of us have observed.

BLOTS

Blots are unresolved single feelings or incidents, such as the emotional shock of experiencing a car accident, the shock horror and disbelief of seeing, or being involved in, a tragic incident. This can be an event of world significance, or it can purely personal. It can be big or small. We can all remember big shocks from world events. Each of us carries, in our Shadow, a myriad of little blots, and some big ones.

May I share a couple of short stories about blots?

One of my daughters stayed an extra year at Primary School, because she was young. One day, at the swimming pool, her former classmates and friends walked past her and ignored her. Frances was understandably upset, a feeling which persisted into the evening. Taking a sequence of flower essences enabled her then to reflect on the incident, to relive and relieve, and finally resolve the series of unresolved emotions that had piled up – 'They don't like me, so I'm unworthy, I'm useless, I'm not lovable, I'm not confident, I'm not going out again, I'm not going swimming again, nobody loves me, I feel separate, I feel unloved, why should I love myself' Frances didn't tell me what she was feeling, we just chose the essences intuitively, and melted each layer of frozen emotion as it came up. After a dozen or so essences, the morose upset pitiful child had been replaced by a smiling happy one. She had resolved and integrated that experience into her life, and could now face the world with confidence again.

An incipient blot, that could have festered and produced a lack of confidence, had been painlessly processed. I'm not suggesting that most single blots can have a major effect – although some certainly can, such as a car accident, or a major personal trauma. In fact, it seems as though a number of blots can, over a period of time, produce a stain.

Another brief story comes from my own Shadow. I was quietly using the Emotional Stress Release technique on day to look at my childhood. Out of nowhere suddenly came an intense feeling of shame – and a memory of doing a poo in my pants when I was seven years old. It had happened near the end of the school day, I'd hung on too long to get to the toilet, and suddenly I realised what I'd done. Too distressed to tell the teacher, my mother uncovered my shame on the way home by asking what that dreadful smell was! Thirty-five years later, the memory popped up – or perhaps pooped up! – whilst I was in what I call Search-and-Heal mode!

BYTES

Bytes are little personal issues, which are just tiny little blots. One caught me out the other day – and made me laugh when I realised it! At a meeting, the presenter was charming and effective. I found myself becoming deeply interested in both the presentation and the presenter. There was something very familiar about her energy. The meeting finished, and we've not met since. Later that evening, I suddenly realised that the presenter looked very similar to the first girl I had ever had a crush on, in my early teens. This is surely a case of projection of powerful positive emotions if ever there was one – though quite amusing to uncover. It showed me some of my un-resolved teenage emotions.

Sometimes bytes surface and can be articulated, usually in the form of a facial expression, and words such as 'I don't want to. . .' or 'I don't like. . .' etc. There are thousands and thousands of these tucked away inside every one of us, to do with blockages from the recent past, our deep past, child-hood, and other times and spaces.

Examples are

* I don't want to play
* I don't want to be involved
* I don't want to be hurt (again)
* I don't want to go to work
* I don't want to go to school

* I don't want to be responsible
* I don't want to hurt you
* I didn't mean to hurt you
* I didn't like that
* I don't like it (whatever 'it' is)
* I can't do it (whatever 'it' is)
* I mustn't do it (whatever 'it' is)

These bytes of feelings, little bits of blots, can often be accessed when they are near the surface of our Shadow. One method is to put your hand on your forehead, as in the Emotional Stress Release Technique, and just allow yourself to articulate your feelings.

There are also even deeper blots hidden within the human psyche. These relate to mythology, Arthurian legend, Judaeo-Christian tradition and all ancient story traditions, some peaceful, some violent. Archetypally we each carry many roles in our psyche. Archetypally

* we have all murdered
* we have all been murdered
* we have all died in childbirth
* we have all died in infancy
* we have all violated another's personal space
* we have all been victims of violation
* we have all died on the Cross
* we have all been a wounded healer
* we have all committed foul deeds
* we have all shirked our responsibilities
* we have all loved
* we have all fulfilled our purpose

Within the collective human psyche, all these roles are held, and each can be accessed, worked through, and healed, whether or not we have in this lifetime experienced the event. (I hope not, for most of the list above.) If we have unwittingly 'rattled any cages' by talking about these sensitive subjects, it serves to illustrate that we each have a deep sensitivity, deep wounds – and with that, as a human, comes also the ability to Heal, to Experience, Express, Resolve and Integrate the experience into our library.

One of the most curious I met recently with a friend, Jack. We'd discussed the list above, and I mentioned the byte 'I don't want to come to this planet', 'I don't want to be born' or 'I don't want to be here' and other similar ones. Jack, an experienced Shaman and journeyer felt a deep resonance with 'I don't want to be born into this life'. And the beauty is, of course, once the unresolved byte is uncovered, it can rapidly be resolved by one of a number of techniques (see Keep Cleansing, Stay Grounded).

It's my guess that we each have millions and billions of experiences, and that quite possibly a large number end up as blots of unresolved memory, hidden away, a little like 'bad areas' on your computer's hard disk! And, I'm sure, just as a computer can mend and defragment its hard disk, it is open to each of us to allow ourselves to enter Search-and-Heal mode – when the time is right, of course!

STAINS

Stains are emotional colourings that affect a whole area or segment of our lives. We each have many stains that are very personal to us, and relate to our individual experiences. Personal stains, like blots, can be accumulated in this lifetime. They can also exist, yet appear to have no obvious origin. In this case, we may presume that if they are personal issues, then they come from other times and other spaces.

We also carry generic stains that are common to whole families, tribes, races or to humanity. Such might be family habits, or tribal prejudices, racial idiosyncrasies, or deep issues that relate to being a human being. These generic stains, common to large groups of people come from the present and the past.

Let's look at some of the personal issues first. Stains can be big or small, but one of the common causes of a larger stain is a bereavement, or a relationship change such as a divorce. Most of us have lost a loved one, perhaps a parent or a grandparent years ago, and went through a period of sadness and unhappiness as a result. Some of us may experience bitterness and resentment. At the time we had these feelings, we may not have had the support to resolve them, either fully or even partially, so we put them into our Shadow for later processing. The way I look at stains is in terms of flower essence pictures. This is a little bit of a cheat, really, because instead of counselling and trying to define the issue, I ask intuitively 'Is there a balanced flower essence combination to help this person for their highest good?' I could equally ask 'How may I best help this person with homeopathy, with orthodox medicine, with healing, with counselling, etc?' but my personal palette to paint from is flower essences as a starting point. In doing this for many people, certain patterns come up time and again. (Now, please don't remind me that's because I am subconsciously projecting my own patterns of imbalance in order to find my personal answers as well – because you're quite right. But can we deal with this in Keep Cleansing, Stay Grounded.)

Patterns that seem to come up are Gorse, Mustard, Walnut, Wild Rose for a bereavement or divorce with just sadness, and Gorse, Mustard, Walnut, Willow for one with considerable resentment as well as sadness. It's often possible to pinpoint these patterns as relating to a particular time e.g. a two-year span of time centred about ten years ago. The yellow Gorse flower brings hopefulness, dissolving hopelessness, whilst taking the Mustard flower essence lifts any clouds of gloom. Walnut is the link-breaker and helps us remain stable and secure inside during times of major change. Wild Rose lifts sadness, whilst Willow helps resolve patterns of 'It's not fair' – or even frank bitterness or resentment. Usually, taking the flower essence combination will resolve the stain over a period of time, and any others that are related.

This is one of the best descriptions I know of what happens when you dissolve a stain with flower essences, a gentle and relatively easy way to do it. See if you can put Accept, Acknowledge, Forgive, Release and Move On into their proper places. You may also note how the Map of Emotional Resolution applies, to see how emotions have been blocked in the past. See how Pamela describes how she Relived, Relieved, Resolved and Integrated issues.

'To begin with the Remedies (Mustard and Walnut) did not seem to be having a noticeable effect. Then I began to notice that various events or occasions in my life would come to mind. Often I would rethink these occasions, see what was really good in them for me and feel much more at ease with the thoughts.

'This happened not only to the good memories but to the bad ones as well. It was as if someone had opened the emotional filing cabinet and no way could I close it. Gradually I have found incident after incident coming to mind for reassessment, memories which at one time I could never have faced again, memories which I could not under any circumstances have shared with anyone could be dealt with and put away. Pandora's box of personal memories was revealing the bad things and gradually each was being cleaned away.

'In this process I learned to really cry again and not to withhold my feelings and batten them down. As a child my mother had insisted that my father never saw me in tears, but now the tears could flow freely. There was no guilt feeling about crying now.

'As the gentle cleansing and healing process has gone on over the weeks I have begun to realise that I am still an attractive woman with a lot to contribute to the world I live in.

'The whole effect seems to me to be rather like an old Dutch master's portrait which has become grimy and soiled with time and smoke from the fire. When it is gently cleaned and restored with modern techniques the beauty of the picture is almost better than in its original state; the lights and tones shine through much more clearly, the subtle hues and highlights become more apparent.'

Of course, if I were a homeopath I would see these stains in terms of Nat Mur for buried grief, inability to cry, Ignatia for grief and distress bubbling up to the surface, or Staphisagria for buried resentment – or one of many other homeopathic remedies available.

Lucy was bullied at school for 'being fat', and developed an eating disorder. She was being sick frequently. Lucy certainly wasn't fat, but the criticism got to her. At seventeen she was a young adult, and was growing out of the uncertainties of adolescence. This is a crucial time of developing self-worth and self-esteem. Unfortunately for Lucy, her parents had recently split up and her mother remarried. Lucy and her stepfather did not see eye-to-eye, nor did she get on well with her mother. You can see that it was difficult for Lucy to develop self-esteem in this atmosphere – in fact, it had plummeted. This allowed her to be easy prey for any criticism. As she sat telling me this story, tears kept welling up. Pine is the essence for self-worth, health and vitality, dissolving negative feelings of guilt and low self-esteem. As I put a drop of the Pine flower essence on her wrist, Lucy found herself unable to stay in the feeling of low unhappiness. The vibrational catalyst supported her like a tuning fork to re-harmonise her perception. Each dose, of course, initially gave effect for a few minutes. Lucy then left home to stay with another family member. Taking Pine over the next few weeks transformed her outlook, whilst Cherry Plum helped her stay in control. Gorse melted sadness, Walnut protected her against the emotions and expectations of her mother and stepfather, whilst Wild Oat helped her find new direction in life. But overall, Pine dissolved the main stain on Lucy's life, which was guilt, lasting about five years. Pine is for guilt. Taking it builds self-esteem. Tellingly, Lucy's sister said 'Of course, mum's always using a guilt trip to keep Lucy under control'.

Stains are rather like onion skins. Beneath one layer of stain, there is often another, which comes to the surface when the outer is resolved. This may be a sadness layer, but may be an angry one, a hurt one, a puzzled one, a dreaming one, or any one of many.

Julie runs a successful business and family. However, even in her thirties, she found going to see her mother emotionally very painful. She'd not found childhood easy for many reasons. Like many she had a painful, bitter adolescence, was bullied and never told her mum or dad. It wasn't until she was eighteen that her mother dropped the bombshell. She said, 'If I had my life over again, I wouldn't have had you.' Julie's mother had been all set for a career after university, when she found herself pregnant almost immediately she married. Her career was blocked. Julie described her relationship with her mother as an adult as 'interesting and rocky'. Whenever she went to see her mother, she would take Ignatia 6c every two or three hours, which would help resolve the mixed feelings of distress that bubbled up to the surface. Julie told me 'You don't choose your mum and dad – you learn to live with them.'

Stains can come from a sequence of lots of similar blots – for instance months of persistent bullying or unhappiness. The origin of some stains is easy to find. Trouble is, as with blots, tangles and cobwebs, they're all invisible to us. It's not until either we work intuitively, or someone or something presses one of our 'hot buttons' or sensitive spots, that we can see that there is a stain at all.

Lessons are often given to us in three different ways, as I found out one morning from three separate patients who came to see me. The lesson was about circumstances that resonate with hidden stains. The first was the time of year. Lynne always felt sad in May, despite the fine weather. Ten years before, her father had been ill and finally died of cancer in May, so this month always held unresolved emotions for her. The second was about the time of pregnancy. Yvonne was pregnant, and initially thrilled. But now, approaching twenty-four weeks gestation (full term is forty weeks), she was becoming distinctly edgy and verging on panic attacks. The trigger was that her first son had been stillborn at twenty-six weeks which explained her apprehension and anxiety. Jan's stain, the third, related to her mother's remarriage. This brought up some strong emotions regarding her father's early death in tragic circumstances, even though this happened eight years ago.

Personal stains can come from other times and places. I have a good friend, Kate, who is a very loving and generous person. She has not travelled outside Europe, however for some unknown reason, she has a deep anger against the – well, I won't say which – race. Suffice it to say, she's never been there or met anyone from that race. However, only a few generations ago, that race oppressed and wiped out one with which she feels great kinship. Indeed, in a daydream once Kate felt that she had been a member of that second race in another time and another space. Figment of imagination or not, but it is true for Kate.

There are certain trigger sounds and words that retold in appropriate circumstances, seem to resonate with stains in our Shadows. If you have a group of healers, for instance, and the conversation drifts to details of Red Indian culture, Aboriginal sacred places, sacred sites around the world, or the place names of sites of trauma in the Languedoc in the South of France at the time of the suppression of the Cathars, then some people may feel distinctly uncomfortable or sad. This may be an indication of a deep buried trauma, deep within the psyche, from another time and space. If you press this further, and intuitively seek a date of personal trauma in the past, it can really strike a deep chord with some of us. However, please may I give a note of caution. It is only appropriate to allow a buried trauma to surface if you are completely prepared and in a fit state to deal with all the issues that may come up. Whether the trauma is from this life or another time and space, if it surfaces, it is relived in order to be relieved. This can on rare occasions be very painful and physically dangerous, by provoking rage, severe anxiety or an asthma attack, amongst other phenomena. That's not a problem if you've got all the tools ready to deal with it – but be prepared! And make sure you're completely clear yourself before trying to help another, otherwise you'll suddenly find yourself dealing with your own stuff as well!

Family stains merge into tribal, depending on whether they come from a small family unit, or a larger group. Military organisations in particular can foster tribal views that can manifest as stains and imbalances in later life. There is of course a very important reason for imprinting the way of thinking in the first place – tribal security. Family stains may be trivial, such as a habit of always doing things one way, without thinking about it. They may also be major, as in patterns of alcoholism and abuse that perpetuate generation after generation. Of course, they express as personal issues, but the origin is family.

The tribe is a powerfully protective unit that bring security to its members – seen particularly in grazing animals who herd together for protection. Humans congregate together and share certain views of the world.

The prevailing Western World view since the Cartesian split of mind from body is a scientific one. Despite much valuable scientific research and progress, there is a mindset of physical materialism deeply imbued in Western culture, as opposed to the more holistic Eastern mind-body view of the world. If you discuss these issues at a scientific level, sooner or later you can meet a block in some people. And the blockage is rarely a rational one – you can tell by the facial expression and emotion that the blockage is a stain – a pattern of imbalance in the way of looking at the world, which has been unconsciously absorbed through schooling. Having had enough of my own prejudices challenged as a scientist, and observed my own (occasionally hysterical) emotional reaction, I think I can confidently say that we all carry many stains that are tribal and racial.

Deeper stains that affect the whole of humanity are gender issues. I'm not quite sure where gender differences come in, but let's make them issues that come up under stains for the time being. There are gender differences between masculine and feminine attributes. You could argue that the ideal perfect human being has a balance of masculine and feminine within, whatever the physical body they wear.

However, we all start from where we are – and there are definite inner differences, partly dictated by the female hormone oestrogen, and the male testosterone.

Masculine attributes are those of the hunter-gatherer, the planner, related to the left-brain analytical skills. Feminine attributes are those of intuition, listening, knowing, nurturing and mothering. These are more related to the right-brain intuitive talents.

Both genders can of course fight, perhaps the male animal with more aggression, the female only when her nest and babies are threatened – but then with tooth and nail.

How does this relate to stains? Well, gender attributes may be beneficial, but they can also act as baggage at times that prevent us from seeing the whole picture. Part of the challenge of life is to evolve as far as we can – and, sooner or later, we each come up against gender issues that are holding us back.

Of course, there are many gender issues that make up the spice of life – I'm all for these, but a few are a problem. You might want to guess that the high sex drive of the adolescent male is an issue for him to resolve – I could not possibly comment!

Even deeper stains are the way we treat our world and our fellow man. I think, although it is impossible to be certain about these things, that such stains include the archetypal Seven Deadly Sins: Pride, Wroth, Envy, Lust, Gluttony, Avarice and Sloth. Certainly there are other stains that are part of being human – animal behaviour such as fear of snakes and fear of spiders are examples. This is likely to be a fruitful research area in the years to come!

TANGLES

Every human being has an energy field around them. When two humans interact in any way, from a glance or a passing thought, to close physical contact, a connection is made. However briefly, the two energy fields are shared, and invisible emotions may pass from one to another. The invisible emotions passed are felt by every doctor, nurse, and mother, and anyone else who listens or cares. Every therapist has had a patient say after a long and deep consultation 'I feel so much better', and the therapist thinks 'I don't – why do I feel so exhausted?' Well, what has happened is an invisible exchange of energy – the patient's troubles (energy imbalance) has been transferred to the therapist, whilst the therapist has allowed their positive energy to be drained away.

Tangles, however, are not so much the energy transfer, as an energy connection, whether by thought or by touch. During this connection, a dialogue is set up. This dialogue/ conversation/interaction/relationship, however brief, ends in due course. The dialogue will either end harmoniously ('business all finished') or inharmoniously, with leftover unfinished business. And when the two people move apart, their energy fields separate.

However, if there *is* unfinished business, there is still an energy connection left intact. Some call it a karmic connection, in the sense of an unresolved issue.

This leaves what we'll call a karmic thread – not in any deep sense of responsibility for world issues, but just because there is unfinished personal business, however insignificant.

Karmic threads or attachments of unfinished business are particularly formed when one, or both, individual has emotions invested in the interaction. You can see that we don't make karmic threads (often) with the people we pass in the street, or meet whilst shopping, but when it comes to more personal issues, we have more at stake. With more at stake, we invest more emotion, and if emotion is invested into an interaction or we enter with an emotional imbalance, then it may be difficult for the relationship to finish tidily.

Threads – or tangles – persist, because we've all got lots and lots and lots of them. They last, they stay, they can last generations, and they can transcend time and space. They persist forever unless they are brought to the light of day and resolved. Fortunately the resolution process can be as simple as forgiveness with love – a process we'll look at in more detail in Keep Cleansing, Stay Grounded.

Many are the tangles created in family and work interactions. Any transaction (the unit of relationship) that does not end cleanly and fairly creates a thread. So when you get upset with your partner, angry with the children, or the government!, or kicked out, you create a karmic thread, part of a web of tangles.

Anne was happy in her relationship, with her son Brian from a previous marriage. However, she held unhappy memories (stains) about Brian's father, who had been an alcoholic and physically violent toward her on many occasions. Tangles had been created. Anne did a quiet forgiveness meditation with her eyes closed. She visualised herself and Brian's father, and asked to see the karmic attachments between the two of them. There are several ways to melt these cold, painful threads – but the key point is to use love. Anne thought she was doing very well, using a small candle flame of love to gently burn off each thread, and its attachment into his and her chakras (mainly solar plexus and sacral) when suddenly her face dropped. She looked aghast and confessed, 'Oh my God – I've set fire to him!' Luckily she was able to mend the intention quickly, and heal any wounds with love. This showed her that even though your intention may be a loving release, you may still have strong emotions trapped inside you, which need gentle release and resolution. Accept, Acknowledge, Forgive, Release, Move On. Experience, Express, Resolve, Integrate.

Many are the tangles we all carry from interactions we know about. As children grow up, become self aware, and transit adolescence, there are so very many opportunities for parents (and the children) to trip up, in however tiny a way, in their relationships. It's a pretty impressive challenge to stay in balance as a parent. Which reminds me of the story about God walking in the Garden of Eden. He'd just created Adam and Eve, and was pleased to see how unsophisticated and unselfconscious they were. God now made a small mistake. OK, it was only a tiny one, but it had pretty profound effects. Instead of encouraging them to do only positive things, he said 'Hi, how are you doing?' 'Fine' they replied. 'Well', said God, 'Just over there is the tree of knowledge – whatever you do, please do *not* eat any of the apples from it'. Now, you know as well as I do, that the subconscious mind just doesn't hear the 'nots'. If I ask you *not* to think of a yellow elephant, what's the first thing that comes into your brain? Sure, yellow elephants! So what did Adam and Eve do? About twenty minutes later, God strolled by. Adam and Eve were enjoying an apple snack. So God said 'I knew it! You've disobeyed me, destroyed my trust. Well, there's only one punishment for you both – from henceforth, you shall bear children, and enjoy the privilege of a household of teenagers.'

Philip and his brother both had families. The cousins played well together. At every family gathering, Philip, though he loved his sister-in-law dearly, always found that he would find fault with her and fall out over a small detail. Never anything important. Once it was over the magazine his seven-year-old bought. 'Pop magazines now – it'll be heroin next' said his sister-in-law. Of course the answer would have been to use humour such as 'Well, if the Spice Girls are their only heroines, it won't really matter!' But Philip was caught up in a tangle. Reviewing it later, he could find no origin from any event. But when a counsellor suggested that he was reacting to an issue from another time and space – a past life if you want to argue that way – he immediately saw an issue and forgave it. Curiously, their relationship has been much easier ever since!

Many are the errors we've all committed with one another, but if we wish, it's not too difficult to sort out the difficulties and start to unweave the tangles we've knotted ourselves into.

Cobwebs

These can be thought of as bits of invisible psychic junk. They can be attached to people, or lie around certain places, surrounding the whole earth with the capacity of infesting, infecting, or infiltrating any other being. A bit similar to the way radio and television transmissions surround us and even pass through us.

Cobwebs are coherent masses of vibrational energy, just as we are – but they are invisible to our eyes. We can, however, sense them and often feel that something is not quite right.

Many people have the ability to sense the vibes of a place – they may feel good or they may not. This intuitive gift is a feminine attribute, though a man can also have it. Often, if a place doesn't feel right, it can be due to cobwebs, either emotional or sometimes psychic.

A while back, I walked into an emotional cobweb. Let me explain. On holiday, I felt quite relaxed. The Cornish coast was beautiful, the weather fine. The walk to fetch a newspaper took me a mile along the cliff and into the bay. A hundred yards from the shop, I started to feel a little uncomfortable. As I came closer, I started to know that something was badly wrong. I sensed fear, though could not trace its source. The dramatic answer came as I walked into the shop. There, on the newsstand, were many colour front pages, with the tragic scene of Concorde airborne, yet in flames, over Paris. The rest of the news story is well known. But what I had sensed was the cobweb consisting of the fear, shock and horror dropped by every reader, both in the shop and as they walked away, stunned by the news. When emotional cobwebs are intense, as this one was, it can be enough to provoke a panic attack in someone who is susceptible – or whose Shadow is nearly full to overflowing. Makes you wonder what negative emotional cobwebs surround us all, transmitted by news stations, and unpleasant films that contain violent and upsetting scenes. Now, I'm not saying you shouldn't live over a newsagents – just that it's worth being aware, so you can put your personal protection on before allowing the vibes to get at you!

An emotional cobweb of a very different kind affected Rhona. She came to me very upset. Reading her intuitively, it seemed that the Bach Flower Remedies Star of Bethlehem for shock and Rock Rose to dissolve terror, were exactly appropriate. (Both are contained in Rescue Remedy and it's counterparts, Emergency Essence and Five Flower & Recovery Remedy). Rhona took them for ten days and came back to see me. She was as distressed as before. I'd obviously forgotten to ask why she was distressed! So I did – and the answer came 'I keep getting the same nightmare'. Being nosy, I asked what the nightmare was 'Aunty's trying to get out of her coffin'. Now, Rhona's aunt had died a few months before. Though not my patient, I had sent her to hospital for the last few days. She had been dying of cancer which she'd hidden from her family and, I think, from herself. Aunty had been born and grown up in the house which was now Rhona's. In essence, she had left her physical body but was definitely still earthbound, trapped. Trapped perhaps by karmic attachments but, much more likely, I think, because she had no belief of life beyond the earth plane.

Fortunately, help was at hand. A priest knew how to guide Aunty to the light, asking her to look for her parents and family who had already passed over. The change in Rhona after this brief ceremony was dramatic. She instantly regained her normal bubbly self, no longer troubled by a cobweb, a cobweb which had attached itself to her.

Some people are particularly vulnerable to this sort of attachment, especially those with auras weakened by disease, or damaged by drugs or alcohol. Certain occupations are also hazardous! For instance, doctors and priests often have contact with the dying. A soul leaving a body with no intention or knowledge of moving into the light can attach itself either to a relative, to someone involved with the death or funeral or even to someone at random.

Stories of near-death experiences have given us lots of pointers to the fact that there is a hereafter, and that when we pass over we are drawn to an incredible light, to a transcendent beauty and stillness. However, in a secular society, many of us are conditioned to believe that we are mere hunks of living meat, waiting to drop off the perch, with nothing beyond death. Holding such beliefs in life, it is difficult to transcend them in death. So it is useful to remember always to look for the light. In death, especially, remembering to look for the light can be a great comfort to the dying loved one.

You can imagine, having heard about Rhona's cobweb and the cobweb near the newsagent, why many battlefields, Red Posts (where hanging of criminals occurred), and some houses have uncomfortable vibes. Sometimes the vibes can be quite malevolent, consisting of not only emotional trauma, stuck souls, but other entities and patterns of psychic imbalance.

Now just as you wouldn't dream of leaving the washing up (of course not!) so there's a bit of a task cobweb clearing here and there. But before your enthusiasm gets the better of you – firstly, none of us have to get involved! Secondly, being aware of something does *not* make you responsible for dealing with it! And thirdly, make sure you're wearing a seatbelt, driving on the correct side of the road, refuelled, with the whole vehicle in tiptop condition if you are going to become involved at all.

Other cobwebs are more generic ones. You could argue that the Seven Deadly Sins that we put into the Stains category are cobwebs. In a way they are, for they have such a powerful hold on the collective unconsciousness that the thought forms that represent them are ever present all around us. Around us, ready to invade us or express themselves if our defences are down or if our energy is low.

There are probably many other thought forms, fears, upsets, worries, each with specific attachments. In *They Shall Expel Demons*, Pastor Derek Prince talks about these negative patterns of imbalance or spirits or demons. He names each of them, and calls them 'your invisible enemies'. He graphically describes the story of a young man who was ensnared by demons, his realisation that he had patterns of imbalance within them, and that no one could help him. He then discovered the ministry of deliverance, was delivered of 'demons' and subsequently became an authority and pastor of deliverance ministry.

When I read Derek's book, I was reminded of a student friend. A hard-drinking, full-blooded medical student, Jim developed M.E. (myalgic encephalomyelitis) after some years in practice.

His energy wasted away. He spent six months in bed, cared for by his parents, barely able to get to the bathroom, unable to stagger downstairs. Jim came to stay with us when he had recovered. His sleep pattern was disturbed, he ate curious combinations of food that he craved at various times of day, and spent long periods just sitting quietly in the garden. His energy level was very low. Jim summoned up the energy to go on holiday with friends. Soon after, he relapsed completely, and spent another few months in bed, cared for by his parents.

Now Jim is one of few people I have seen completely cured from M.E., or post-viral fatigue syndrome. He is also someone who has had full investigation and confirmation of the illness, under a leading professor.

How did Jim get better? Through healing, through his sister's church. As a former medical student friend, Jim was almost embarrassed to confide in me, thinking I might not believe, or that he might offend my beliefs. Jim was lying in bed, when his sister offered healing. After several sessions of church healers laying on hands in his bedroom, Jim was just strong enough to attend church. In a healing service, Jim went up to the front for deliverance and healing, in the name of Christ Jesus. He experienced strange jerkings and contortions. His face twisted, and he belched and sneezed. After a few minutes of these phenomena, Jim felt strangely at peace, and rather better than before.

Jim was soon able to return to work, and has since married and had a family. He has also developed a strong, unshakeable faith as to the source of his healing, and directed his life accordingly. He has remained fit and healthy ever since.

Now, I am sure there are many causes of M.E., and that it is possible that Jim's healing is an unusual story. It's also possible that he was only capable of being healed because he had parental support, good nutrition, and many other positive factors. I'm certainly not suggesting that most cases of M.E. can be healed in this way. Yet this story stuck in my mind, so that when I came across Derek Prince's work on Deliverance, it rang a very loud bell.

Jim told me that for him, the key was Alignment. He aligned himself to Jesus Christ as his Saviour, as part of God, the Three-in-One: Father, Son and Holy Spirit. From that point, the Holy Spirit filled him and there was no longer any room for any imbalance, let alone any 'unclean spirits'.

Alignment, Balance and a deep knowing of Connection, that allows us to be filled with the Universal Carrier Wave of Unconditional Love, or the Holy Ghost, if you wish. And if we are filled with balance and harmony, there is no space for patterns of imbalance. At least until the next learning experience of what's in our Collective Shadow! And at the point when we are filled with balance and know our connection, it is easier to display the Christlike talents of loving, knowing, healing and creating that are within each of us, waiting to manifest, as we allow ourselves to be guided by the Holy Spirit (as opposed to any unholy or unclean spirits) working through us. As the closing blessing often says

'May the peace of God, which passes all understanding, the love of our Lord Jesus Christ, and the Holy Spirit, enfold and infill you, and go with you on your journey'.

There are probably 'unclean spirits' i.e. patterns of imbalance that can space-share our vibrational body, if we allow them to. And, as human beings, we all have potential susceptibility in our make-up. In space-sharing, these patterns of imbalance can cause many manifestations from strange, intrusive thoughts, out-of-character habits and obsessions, lusts, to tics, grimaces, belching and flatulence.

Before you read the next section, please just affirm your connection to Source, and let the Divine Light flood through you. Such 'spirits', if we name them thus, include negative imbalances such as spirit of hate, spirit of anger, spirit of cancer, spirit of lust, spirit of pornography, spirit of frustration, spirit of intolerance, spirit of war, spirit of lying, spirit of mistrust, spirit of doubt, and so on.

It seems that all these 'spirits' are thought forms that have a life – or at least an existence of their own. They are fed by negative thoughts and fears that human beings put out. It is fear that feeds them. Resolve, courage and confidence do **not** feed them. Resolve, courage and confidence, a deep inner knowing, and a deep feeling of connection to Source, or the Godforce, dispel and dissolve them.

Alignment, Balance and Connection to the Source seem to magically make all cobwebs and Shadows vanish like wisps of morning mist when sunshine falls upon it.

'Spirits' i.e. negative thought forms, can only affect us if we are susceptible to them. That is to say, if our vibrational integrity is not intact, or if there are chinks in our armour. In essence, separation from the Source at one level or another can allow fear to develop. And we remember from earlier, that fear is the dark room of our lives where we process the negative.

Now, in the Bible, we're told that Jesus performed Deliverance. In fact, his ministry was threefold – Healing, Teaching and Deliverance. Jesus acknowledged that there could be a problem in casting out one demon – because seven more might enter. The point he was making here is Susceptibility. We can only be susceptible to invasion or space-sharing (a) if we allow it (consciously or subconsciously) and (b) if we have a vibrational imbalance somewhere in our soul that permits it to happen. So deliverance goes hand-in-hand with healing, with sealing the aura, with mending leaks and tears.

If we have a weak aura, or imbalances, it may be possible for a whole wraithlike stuck soul to space-share our vibrational energy pattern. This is a well-known phenomenon that can occur to people with a drugs or alcohol problem. They are fine whilst they stay off the substance. When they first take some, it acts as a partial poison, loosening the hold of the etheric on the physical body. At this point, you are more susceptible. Next, the following scenario can happen, such as with an addicted alcoholic: 'I only intended to have just one drink, but after one, it was as if something got into me. I can't remember a thing after that – they tell me I just drank and drank all evening'. Possibly what is happening is:

Normal person (some imbalances – after all, we all have them!)
susceptible
but safe whilst avoiding the trigger

trigger (e.g. alcohol, sleep depletion, illness)
unsafe – vulnerable
vibrationally permits space-sharing
'spirit of drunkenness' – or old Joe Soap
the well-known deceased alcoholic (still
earthbound)
invades our friend
leads to
'out of character' behaviour
in this case – drunkenness

It seems that given the right trigger, we can all be susceptible – so it's worth looking for our patterns of imbalance and healing them. More in Keep Cleansing, Stay Grounded. When people have some of these space-sharing entities leave them, there can be very visible physical manifestations of the change in pattern. These include belching, retching, diarrhoea, flatulence, yawning, gasping, and contortions, shakings and jerkings. And sneezes – don't forget sneezes! Bless you!

In summary: we all have a Shadow that contains all our patterns of imbalance, all our unresolved issues. It contains blots and bytes – the unresolved emotion of events and unresolved simple negative thought forms, and stains – emotional imbalances covering a larger area. These can be personal present, personal recent, personal past, personal other times and spaces, gender, familial, tribal, social or of humanity. We also find tangles, unresolved issues in relationships with other people, and cobwebs – bits of invisible psychic junk – whether an emotion stuck to a place, an earthbound soul, stuck to a place or to a person, or 'unclean spirits' – negative thought forms either generalised or intensely personal which can stick to either people or places. All of these are different patterns of imbalance – ways in which we can deviate from the perfection of our potential, that potential when we are Aligned, Balanced and in Connection. How do we find what's in our Shadow – and how do we deal with it?

We can't if we deny it, nor if we don't help each other.

Remember that we attract a Resonance in other people, which shows us our own unresolved issues – it's easier to look at others' Shadows – so let's help each other, and help ourselves. The first thing we can do is to suspend judgment, and start Accepting. We can then Acknowledge, Forgive, Release and Move On.

CHAPTER 6

Keep Cleansing, Stay Grounded

In this chapter we shall look at ways to help us heal parts of our Shadow, ways to keep ourselves in balance and some simple techniques of healing. These techniques can of course be used on others as well as yourself.

If this book was a mystery novel, then I suppose this chapter ought to be the denouement, the part where all the answers slot into place, the pieces of the jigsaw fit together, and the reader can smile with satisfaction at the way the story has neatly ended.

Well, it's not a mystery novel, and the story isn't going to end that neatly. Or is it? You see, life is actually a journey of experiences, a series of word-searches, a sequence of puzzles, a never-ending jigsaw. Perhaps life is even a mirror where the outside world, and our experiences and bodies, give us clues as to our degree of inner harmony, or as to where the next blot, byte, stain, tangle or cobweb lies.

If you want to end as perfection, with all the pieces in place, I'm not sure we reach it in any one lifetime. Anyway, if you do reach perfection, every experience completed and integrated, no Shadow left, no baggage remaining, then it's probably time to graduate from the earth plane!

Remember how the small child picks up skills – walking, talking, reading, writing, riding a bike – and gets encouragement at every stage? Well, perhaps the invisible journey of emotional maturity and resolution of our personal Shadow and humanity's general Shadow deserves the same enthusiastic approach and encouragement. And some gratitude! An Appreciation and Support Culture, rather than an atmosphere of blame. How often do we get up and say thank you for the day, and for all the other things we take for granted? But it doesn't happen. Because nobody taught us the maps, so we all use denial. And without the maps it's difficult to learn the tools or get started. We've not got the knowledge, the skills, or the attitudes to deal with all the issues, so we go back to using denial instead!

What this chapter can't do is give you all the answers. Sorry about that! The whole area of personal development has been a key growth area for the first half of this century. But what we can do is share some of the ways in which we can find answers to keeping cleansing, staying grounded, and take a look at some of the pitfalls. Let's remind ourselves of the maps we've looked at.

The Ladder of Emotional Healing: Accept, Acknowledge, Forgive, Release, and Move on.

I'm Fine: Fearful, Insecure, Neurotic and Emotionally Imbalanced.

The Map of Emotional Resolution: Experience, Express, Resolve then Integrate.

The mechanism we use to keep issues unprocessed and in our Shadow: Denial.

The means we use to stay in Denial: Repression, Distraction, Avoidance, Projection (outwards or internally) Comfort behaviour, Risk-Taking behaviour, Escape into fantasy, Blotting it out and then when it all gets too much – Overwhelm.

Healing a trauma: Relive, Relieve, Experience, Express, Resolve, Integrate.

Energy transformation: High Vibration – Lower. Spiritual – Physical – Grounded.

Getting in Touch: Alignment, Balance and Connection.

Patterns of Imbalance: Blots, Stains, Tangles, and Cobwebs.

Remember that we're dealing with an invisible world – the world of our emotions and thought forms. The trouble with the invisible is that we can't see it! So, if we don't understand how something happens, we tend to think of it as magic or a miracle. Perhaps a miracle is just a happening whose mechanism we don't understand? And magic is what makes miracles happen? After all, we take the wonders of electricity for granted: electrons moving along wires to give light, wash clothes, provide heating, run a computer, pump water, and so on. But I've never *seen* an electron, so it all could be just a fairy story!

Now, we can all use magic in our lives in many ways. Remember that Energy Follows Thought (and that what you resist persists).

The corollary is that we do well to use our thoughts wisely, in order to manifest our energy wisely. To do that, we do well to have a purity of intention – after all, magic is magic but the only difference between white magic (done for the good of all) and black magic (performed for self gain, power or control) is the Intention with which it is wielded. Control or Empowerment? Which Intention? Control (black magic) or Empowerment and Upliftment (white magic)? We each have a choice, an ability to choose our response, a Response-Ability = Responsibility.

CONSCIOUS INTENTION

Conscious Intention is very powerful. We have seen in Conscious Energy that there is a powerful vibration of harmony in the Creation, so it makes sense at some level to align ourselves with forces of harmony and balance. The alternatives to conscious alignment with harmony and balance are either no conscious intention, or deliberate intention to align with patterns of disharmony and imbalance. And unfortunately, 'no conscious intention' is likely to end up with accidental alignment with patterns of imbalance at times, so it may be worth reviewing our Conscious Intentions.

If Spirituality includes the science of all our invisible bits – our soul, emotions, etc. – then religion acts as enabling mechanisms to allow us to access the deep springs of spirituality within us. Of course religions differ, though the core messages are similar. Love God and love others are the two key tenets of Christianity – other religions are broadly similar. Religions give teachings, provide lessons, and support in developing truth and faith. That religions differ is part of the great learning experience of humanity, not just the politics of spirituality!

It is said that all the answers are deep within us – as are all our abilities to cope. Having seen how modern physics explains things in Conscious Energy, then the mystics and poets are proved right. Especially the *Book of Enoch*, in some versions of the Bible, which has dozens of verses, each ending 'Be Still, and Know I am God'.

Let's remind ourselves of one of the maps.

* Alignment (and Awareness)
* Balance
* Connection

to patterns of balance and harmony in Creation, named as God, the Source or the god-force. These patterns of balance and harmony, made manifest in man, shine out as the Christ-like talents.

So, Conscious Intention

* Alignment
* Balance
* and Connection

What are our main tools to help us still our selves, become aligned and remain connected? Alignment comes through asking, or in religions terms, prayer. Permit me a short story. I have had a fortunate life, with loving parents and family, good food and schooling, and a fortunate 'series of coincidences' that led me to practice medicine, which I love.

Yet, in my early thirties I felt at a crossroads. I have grown up with faith in myself, and faith around me. One day, as a result of a short series of unusual circumstances, I bought and read a book I'd heard about on the radio. At the bottom of page ninety-seven (or somewhere) of this book on spirituality, I read 'If you want to opt in, all you have to do is ask'. Intrigued, next day I started saying quietly to myself something like 'please guide me in the ways of love and Christ, and help me serve'. Now this had a remarkable and profound effect. Life started to move forwards in leaps and bounds. I found myself learning rapidly about flower essences (my passion and hobby), which are powerful tuning forks to rebalance us, about energies, healing, dowsing (a way to ask questions of our Intuition – our In-Tune Station) and so on. It doesn't matter how you ask, or what you use, but essentially the challenge is to be prepared to accept Help and Support – and then ask for it.

And at the point you work with Help and Support – tuned to your Intuition, your In-Tune Station – then things can work very powerfully, and even magically, in your favour.

So be prepared to Ask for Help!

Ask for help from others – accept counselling, accept someone to help you as a coach. This need not be in depth serious stuff – just having a friend, or a professional counsellor, to hold a safe space for you can be incredibly supportive and cathartic. In fact, it is when we feel supported, when there is a safe space, that we can allow painful issues to surface out of our Shadow. In surfacing, they can be Relived, and, supported, Relieved, in order that our unresolved emotion can be Experienced, Expressed, Resolved and Integrated.

Ask within yourself and allow life to bring you the answers. Because when you are Aligned, it's easier to stay calm and centred. If we are calm and centred, we can listen to life's messages, observe events (rather than be embroiled), remain detached, and of course stay grounded. And then we are in Balance – and if Aligned and in Balance, we are automatically Connected to the great patterns of Harmony in Creation, or the god-force, our Higher Selves, however you wish to view it. And Aligned, we are Aware.

It is when we are balanced and still, that we can listen carefully to the messages from within – the small still voice of calm. As Joy Pike puts it:

> For every kind thought, let there be a whisper
> For every kind whisper, let there be a word
> For every kind word, let there be an action
> For every kind action brings the light of God to man

There's one secret tool that helps us stay in balance – and that's breathing. Breathing in balance is a rhythmic flow, a gentle in-pause-out-pause, in-pause-out-pause. When in rhythmic balance in ourselves, it is easy to be in balance with the rhythm flows of the universe. When we breathe gently, deep into our being, with conscious intention, we automatically Balance ourselves. If we are in Balance, we can listen, observe, detach, and become Aware. Sounds airy-fairy, doesn't it? Of course, all the ego excuses start piling in – 'I'm too busy', 'I've got to go to work', 'there are chores to do', 'someone needs me to do. . .', 'I must do. . .'. Well, ego, like a child full of mischief, wants to play the game it's own way – and certainly doesn't want help or the discipline of Balance. Funny thing is, once you do get Aligned, Balanced and (automatically) Connected, the loud voice of ego seems suddenly to have disappeared, which is curious. Unless, of course, you're setting yourself up for a learning experience!

So Balance permits Awareness. And in Awareness we can observe, detach, yet know what is right. We can then choose our Response to life, and act with Conscious Response-Ability. For much of our external life, the events we attract, the characteristics that we admire or that irritate us in the people we meet, acts as a mirror to us, to help us know what is next in the in-tray of Life to deal with. Life is indeed a Mirror of Existence.

Meditation techniques are ways of achieving Balanced, Still Awareness: Awareness not just of external events, but of our own thoughts. Regular meditation is proven to improve our physical health and well-being, so why not learn? After all, we don't have to sit cross-legged quietly voicing the OM (AUM or IAM). We can just quietly observe our breathing as we move through daily life, and make life a waking meditation.

So do try slowing down your breath, and observing it. Fast, shallow breathing is nervous, anxious breathing. Slow, deep breaths are calm, relaxed breaths. Profound inner changes happen to our bodies when we breathe consciously, naturally and rhythmically. Next time you are out of balance, try to notice your breathing pattern – you'll find it interesting!

If we can remain calm and centred, if we can listen, observe, remain detached, and stay grounded, then we can stay in balance.

We looked at Chakras and Energy meridians briefly in Conscious Energy. On the page opposite we have outlined a brief Grounding Meditation for everyday use.

POSTURE AND NUTRITION

After breathing, comes Posture. Some postures make us tense. Think of someone hunched over an office desk. Some postures facilitate anger, others make it impossible! As a quick exercise, feel free to sit up straight, stretch your arms out wide and next bend your elbows, so your hands are above your head, palms open. Now try and feel angry. Can you? Can you really? It's very difficult! Now relax again. Sit forwards a little, frown, fold your arms across your body, clench your fists, hunch your shoulders forward, and try to feel loving and happy! Can you? Well done if you can, it's really not easy! But if you were to reverse the postures you would find the opposite.

So learning about conscious use of our physical frame, and using balancing harmonising postures can be valuable. The Alexander Technique, Tai Chi and Yoga are all aimed to help build harmony in the body. If you're unsure what good posture is, and how to use your body well, just watch the average three-year-old, and take note! Small children use their bodies well, without the constraints of long hours at desks, and with the spontaneity of youth. They also whistle, hum and sing spontaneously – adults take note!

Grounding Exercise

Allow yourself to sit comfortably, legs uncrossed, feet firmly on the floor (or in the Lotus position if this is your third time through the book). Allow yourself to feel a strong connection between the base of your spine and your feet, down into Mother Earth, who provides our physical nourishment. Allow this deep connection to grow stronger, you may perhaps see strong roots growing from your base down into the earth. These roots allow warm nourishment to flood into your body from below, firstly making your feet comfortable and relaxed, then your legs. Next the energy fills your base, sacral and solar plexus Chakras in turn, filling your abdomen with warm loving energy. The warm nourishment now reaches your heart and throat Chakras, filling your chest and arms, before moving on upward to neck and head, filling throat, brow and crown Chakras in turn. Now the flow of warm nourishment continues from below, filling you fuller and fuller, until you are fully nourished and supported. When you are completely full, all the extra coming in from the bottom rises up and flows out of the top of your head, in a gentle fountain, returning back down to earth again, in a warm shower around you. Feel the flow of warmth.

You feel relaxed and comfortable. Allow your consciousness to come back into your body, back to today, to your room. Wriggle your fingers, stretch your toes, and gently when you are ready, allow your eyes to open. How does that feel? It is so important to feel a connection to earth and to stay a clear vessel in order to transform and ground spiritual energy effectively. Too much energy, or blockage, is just as unhelpful a state as too little.

Next, of course, we have to have nourishment for our physical bodies. So, make it a hobby to learn all you can about nutrition, about food quality, about food processing, about additives, about enzymes, minerals and vitamins, about fresh food and vibrancy, about fruit and vegetables, about carbohydrates, about the ways in which food affects us. There are sciences of eating well, such as Ayurveda, as well as our Western knowledge. There are also systems of food combining. Learn to choose food wisely, and trust your intuition.

One intuitive tool that some people use is the pendulum – do you remember the Professor from Hergé's *Adventures of Tintin*? He was always using a pendulum to ask questions about things. A pendulum is merely a tool to produce an outer manifestation of our inner state of tension. If we feel good about something we feel relaxed, and the pendulum moves one way. If we feel bad (even subconsciously) about something, we feel tense, and the pendulum will move a different way. There's the story about the chap who was dowsing in the supermarket recently, asking questions about food quality on a scale of 0-10 and also the appropriateness for his family (again on a 0-10 scale). He was asked to leave by the manager, not because he'd done anything wrong, but because a dozen other people were so fascinated that they were all buying exactly the same things! It played havoc with stock control, the manager explained!

Still on the subject of food and nutrition – if we prepare and eat our food with Alignment, Balance and Connection (love for short), it will be even better for us! Many traditions ask us to bless our food, and say grace – both aiming to raise the vibrations of the food in front of us.

After breathing, posture and nourishment come all the other ways to use (or abuse) our physical bodies – so make it a hobby to keep learning and practising.

THE MIRROR OF LIFE

When it comes to healing our Shadows, if we use the map we're off to a good start. Now, life is often thought to be a mirror, so it will often reflect back to us areas that need attention. If you look around your office and bedroom, and it's full of clutter – ask yourself – is my life full of clutter? If something goes wrong with your car, ask is it significant? Messages my car has given me include 'coolant level low' (watch out for your over-enthusiasm, Andrew), skidding (watch your balance), breaking a door handle (have you got a grip on life?), a wing mirror (look carefully at the effect you're leaving behind you) and so on.

Life can become quite a fun crossword puzzle, or jigsaw. Trouble is, you're not always aware of the clues, even if you're given them – so slow down and take note!

Our physical bodies can also give us messages – this is covered comprehensively by Louise Hay in *You Can Heal Your Life* and Dr Christine Page in *The Mirror of Existence* and *Frontiers of Health*.

Our physical appearances and symptoms can often give us a clue or deeper messages – it gets a bit like a detective story!

One that foxed me was Janet. Janet was ninety years old and developed a red rash over much of her body. None of the creams or medicines I prescribed were of any help – Janet was still affected. A charming lady, she kept her emotions to herself. Three months later, Janet had a stroke and died, leaving a rich life behind her – she'd run a business until she was 88! Talking to her relatives, they confided that her rash had started two days after her sister had been admitted to hospital for her last illness. Janet was very fond of her sister and couldn't express her upset and distress in words, but perhaps her body did it for her.

If you get a pain in the neck, ask 'Is anyone a pain in the neck to me'? If you have low back pain, are you carrying too much load in life? There are many more ways in which physical symptoms can give messages, and a number of books about them. May I just leave you with one last story?

Sarah came in, unhappy and dejected. She was complaining of haemorrhoids (piles). I prescribed some ointment. A month later, she returned with another problem. Anxious to know if she had received benefit from my last prescription, I asked if the ointment had helped. 'No', she said, 'But I've got rid of my husband and that's made me better – he was a right pain in the backside!' (And her piles *had* got better!)

Just as our physical body can act as a Mirror, so too can Life – the Mirror of Existence, as Dr Christine Page calls it.

So far in Keep Cleansing, Stay Grounded, we've looked at some maps, at conscious intention, a the ABC of being in contact with our deep inner selves, at breathing, posture and nutrition.

Let's now turn to our Shadows – Blots, Stains, Tangles and Cobwebs.

ACCEPTING AND TRANSFORMING OUR SHADOWS

The key point here is that if you are aiming to accept rather than deny, to heal rather than suppress, do ask for help. We don't have to do it all alone. It's doing it alone, unsupported, without help, that got us into the mess in the first place. Only when we have the courage to accept our mistakes, to recognise our patterns of imbalance, can we heal them and learn from them. And we all make mistakes. The most humbling words I have ever heard came from a London taxi driver. On my bike I nearly ran into his taxi. You see, he was driving the wrong way up a one-way street. I pulled up sharply, and in my hot-headed youth was about to tell him off. But he got there first. His 'Sorry mate, haven't you ever made a mistake?' disarmed me and completely resolved my anger and irritation.

In what ways can help come? Well, from tools and skills we learn ourselves – listening, detachment, observation, awareness, self-healing, emotional stress release, working with healing tools and tuning forks such as homeopathy or flower essences, neuro-linguistic programming, transformational breathing and so on. And, most importantly, from others in life. We can all help each other and we are all healers. At one end of the spectrum, a sympathetic smile is healing. At the other end, a skilled counsellor, bodyworker, masseur, homeopath, Reiki practitioner, life coach, reflexologist, kinesiologist, doctor, mother, lover, friend, relative (plus all the others I've left out) are all healers.

There are a number of healing tools for stains, including counselling, life coaching, NLP, bodywork and so on.

Counselling and NLP have helped many millions of people review aspects of their lives, reframe them, and in so doing, resolve them. Counselling at its simplest, can be the telling of a story to a best friend, or even a stranger. We've all had the experience of retelling a story to someone else and suddenly realising that we can now see things in a different light. It's when we are able to detach from the emotion that we can see events in a clearer light.

Sometimes the combined effect of lots of stains is that we can lapse into a depression. At this point, antidepressant medication may be valuable to lift us up out of the pit. Counselling, flower essences and other tools can all be used at the same time in order to resolve the issues that helped us into the pit in the first place. Medical therapy and counselling are invaluable at these times, so do consult a medical practitioner if you feel depressed, especially if you have any thoughts of suicide.

If we are overwhelmed repeatedly over a period of time, it is possible to relapse into a numbed sadness, with or without physical symptoms such as poor sleep or a low appetite. If you are in this state for a period of time, some of your brain's neurotransmitters may change, and you may become depressed. It is at this point that it is worth seeking help, and seeing a doctor. Antidepressant medicines can give a chemical boost to the neurotransmitters, and give us a lift. This lift can bring us back to a state where we can function again, and in this lifted state we may be better able to begin to resolve the issues that drove our mood down into depression. However, to use antidepressants as the only solution, without ever trying to resolve the issues that led to the problem, is an incomplete strategy, as it only treats the symptoms and not the causes.

Here we will concentrate on self-help techniques, and changing the vibes. So now we'll talk a little about humour, breathing, emotional stress release, flower essences and homeopathy.

In the safe space that help gives us, issues can surface from our Shadow, and once they have surfaced they can be recognised, acknowledged, relived, relieved, resolved and integrated. There are many, many different techniques that can be used to help. If you're seeing a practitioner, go with the flow of their techniques. If you've got some good techniques of your own, then please (a) use them and (b) share them!

Let's look at some. . .

HUMOUR

Humour is a vital tool. If we can see the funny side of something it diffuses the heaviness and helps resolve it. Some races are better at this than others – some of us are particularly dour and serious, some not.

Laughter is another positive way of resolving emotion, whilst the release of tears can facilitate the resolution or catharsis of all sorts of emotions. Tears can be tears of sadness, tears of self pity, tears of release, tears of pain, tears of resolution or tears of happiness and joy. The five Healing Qualities of Laughter are said to be these

* Laughter reminds us we are bigger than any problem we face.
* Defenceless comedy evokes defenceless laughter.

* Laughter illuminates the Shadow.
* Humour is a mind-altering substance.
* Laughter invites celebration, and reminds us of the joy in life.

BREATHING

As we breathe rhythmically in and out, we reflect the rhythm of the universe, and connect ourselves to its continuous harmonious rhythmic ebb and flow. To do this unconsciously is easy, but at times of stress or shock, we may 'catch our breath', and hold in our reactions and emotions. If, however, we can maintain a steady, constant, relaxed, rhythmic pattern to our breathing, we remain in balance. It is in catching our breath that we trap an issue inside us, unresolved, and give it somewhere to lodge. By breathing steadily and slowly through an issue, we maintain balance, and fail to get enmeshed with unresolved issues or emotions.

Down the ages, many cultures have stressed the importance of right breathing. It is perfected as an art form in practices such as T'ai Chi and Yoga. However, you and I can get a long way just by observing our breath, and ensuring that it is slow and rhythmic. Breathing can also be a therapy.

Transformational breathing involves the use of a therapist to observe your pattern of breathing lying down. Do you breathe shallowly or deeply? Do you breathe into your upper chest, lower chest, or abdomen? By then encouraging you to breath properly, breathing into the constricted areas and using the diaphragm to expand your whole chest, something very curious can happen. Speeding up the breathing for a short while, stuck (unresolved) issues seem to surface out of the Shadow, and can be expressed. A whole chunk of raw emotion can come up – at which point we generally try, out of habit, to repress it – by catching our breath! Continuing to breathe, however, allows the stuck emotion to surface and be expressed – and the common result is a cathartic release of the large chunk of raw emotion.

The way in which this chunk of emotion is released, whilst breathing deeply and lying on the ground, is very like a toddler lying down and having a tantrum! In fact, for this reason, it's called a tantrum – you end up beating your arms and legs up and down, often emitting a loud and throaty roar. And it feels great when you've finished!

Of course, this isn't for everyone – just going for a good workout in the gym, a hard swim, game of squash, or any other hard exercise can have the wonderful cathartic effect of burning off stuck emotion in a controlled way. The beauty of both the exercise and the transformational breathing tantrum technique is that the stuck emotion is being resolved *without* projecting it at someone else – which is what we so often manage to do, even if we don't mean to!

ALIGNMENT AND BALANCE – SAFETY BELTS

Staying in ABC (Alignment, Balance and Connection) is useful – as it gives awareness. There are a couple of safety belts to wear if we are healing ourselves (or others). One is ABC, so always work for the highest good of all. This releases any personal gain from the situation, and allows events to flow for the highest good.

The other morning I picked up the phone. It was an excited Flora. 'Can Rose come and play, please?' Off balance, knowing Rose had homework to do, I answered 'I'm sorry, no. But. . .' But Flora had sensed the block, and had already rung off – her eight-year-old enthusiasm crushed. I should have replied 'Yes, but she has to do her homework first.' Luckily, Rose rang back and was able to play three hours later. It's only too easy to block flow by not thinking before you speak.

Another safety belt is to affirm that you are always in Balance and Grounded. Next affirm your toolkit – I find Stuart Wilde's book *Affirmations* very helpful here: 'I draw from within me everything I need to go beyond my challenges.' That means that you will never have a challenge you are unable to overcome – or, put another way, that we all have a toolkit that can deal with every issue and challenge that comes our way. (Often we may hold mistaken beliefs to the contrary.)

Next point is to be ready and able to deal with anything that comes up in yourself, or your client. Release of trauma patterns can produce some powerful physical symptoms on occasion. So you might like to ask that everything should happen in the perfect space-time sequence, GENTLY! No point in asking for a turbo-charged bumpy ride!

Finally, make sure you're protected – you don't want to pick up someone else's blots or cobwebs. Some people find it very useful to take the Bach flower remedy Walnut for protection – advisable for every therapist, medical or other, because there are many unseen energies that can jump the gap between therapist and client. Another protective tool is to mentally draw or visualise three circles of white light around yourself, and to remember to cleanse your aura regularly. Sue Lilly of Green Man Essences advises in addition to use essences such as Pine and Gorse mixed (Bach), Pennyroyal (Green Man), Labradorite or Black Tourmaline Gem Essences or Crystal Clear from Petaltone Essences. She also recommends using crystals, talismans or commercial protection devices if indicated intuitively.

EMOTIONAL STRESS RELEASE

Now, when it comes to healing an issue, any catalyst that stills us, or reharmonises patterns of imbalance can help.

There's a whole science of techniques such as Emotional Freedom, Acupressure on emotional holding points, and Kinesiology. *Instant Emotional Healing* by Peter Lambrou and George Pratt has some superb advice.

Let's investigate one easy technique – that of Emotional Stress Release. You can use it on yourself or someone else and it is so simple it's laughable. It's brilliant for blots!

We all know the gesture of hand on forehead, or holding your head in your hands when you're stressed or hassled. Well, within this gesture lies an important process – that of Emotional Stress Release, a term coined by Brian Butler of kinesiology fame.

If humans had horns, they would sprout from our frontal eminences, two points on our forehead an inch above our eyebrows. Holding these two points lightly seems to join up a circuit that allows emotional healing to occur.

Remember how an experience can contain painful emotions, and how it can be blocked rather than expressed? Well, holding the ESR points unblocks the blockage, and allows emotions to flow. We all do these unconsciously at moments of stress.

To consciously use this unconscious gesture is one of the most powerful tools we have to hand. It helps us reframe and resolve blots and stains from our Shadows.

However, if we do it when we are not stressed and have no particular current problem, the technique will access whatever blots in our Shadow we choose, or at least the one that's nearest the surface. In using this process we are choosing to relive, and thus relieve a memory and all its associated emotion. Sometimes the emotion is too much so we push it away, much as we might have in the very first place. We can use this process to relive any of our memories, remembered or forgotten, because in turn they are retrieved for reflection, to be relived, relieved, resolved and integrated.

Carol's story will illustrate personal use of ESR, after which we'll look at how to give and to receive it.

'I had been having many physical and eventually psychological problems due to a near fatal accident. As well as suffering from the aftermath of the accident I was also trying to recover from the effects of drugs given to help me cope with the stress and trauma of it all. Andrew explained to me how our minds and body affect each other and are not separate, so it is important to treat the whole person because we can all carry around with us a lot of emotional 'baggage'. Now I must admit all this was very new to me but as I had already used Flower Remedies that he had prescribed as part of my treatment with great success I listened intently. Although I thought it seemed a little too simplistic (the best things often are though) I decided to give it a try. I must admit I was very sceptical. By then I was having some very traumatic memories coming back to haunt me, and didn't think anything so simple could help.

'The first time I tried ESR, I decided that I would deal with the memory of my accident itself and made sure I was not going to be disturbed and began by putting my hand on my forehead and trying desperately to bring this memory forward. Within a matter of seconds I found myself reliving, not the memory of my accident but the day my beloved seventeen year old nephew, Mark, died in a car accident ten years previously. Now this completely threw me. I was struck by the most overwhelming feelings of grief. I cried like a small child. This process went on for quite a while. Afterwards I felt such inner peace and calmness and realised that this 'catharsis' was a essential part of the healing process. Whereas before I couldn't talk about Mark without crying, I can now talk about him quite happily and remember what good times we had.

'What I learnt from this experience though is that I personally couldn't dictate to my subconscious or command a specific memory at will but that they came in their own time. Since that day I have dealt with many other memories including the accident. It's like when you've lost something at home for instance, you'll search and search for it to no avail then one day when you're not looking anymore you find it. Don't go hunting for specific memories – they will find you in their own time. It's like a safety feature to stop you being so overwhelmed with too much too soon. During ESR, the memories and images that come up can take you by surprise if you are not prepared or do not understand that they can seem very real, colours can be bright and vivid. I liken it to having your own home movie running through your mind, to some extent you are the Producer and Director but your subconscious is the editor.

'If you practice ESR you will be able to deal with any past or quite recent memories and traumas in a safe environment and in your own time and reap the benefits. From being very sceptical about it I would now having used it have no hesitation in recommending it to anyone.'

WORKING WITH ESR

Sometimes, what comes up can be overwhelming. At this point, to have someone else do the ESR technique on you is very helpful and supportive. If a baby cries, it has the privilege of being cuddled and settled by mother or by father. It usually settles, receiving the vibrations of reassurance from a powerful source of calm, reassuring love. Babies know how to receive.

Children get cuddled and reassured to a certain extent – but most of us learn not to receive, 'to stand on our own two feet', 'to walk alone'. In not receiving, we lose a valuable source of support and reassurance.

To receive ESR, sit quietly, and allow your eyes to close. To give ESR, first put on your safety belts (as above). You may also use a bubble of golden light, and the Bach flower essence, Walnut, is a powerful protector that all therapists and healers can benefit from. Sipping water with Walnut Flower Essence can insulate us against other people's vibes sneaking in (which they will if you don't).

To give ESR, stand on the receiver's left side. Place your left hand on their forehead and your right over their heart, on their back. The circuit is now complete. Allow yourself to be a channel of whatever healing is to come through you and remember to connect to Source, and be grounded yourself.

As giver, all you have to do is 'hold the space' and make sure that you neither pick up any imbalances from the receiver nor give them! If you're going to offer healing, try to do it when you're in balance yourself – wobbles are infectious. I've certainly picked up enough wobbles from other people!

As receiver, you now have a very curious but reassuring feeling. The first thing that happens is that you feel very calm, very supported, and very safe. It's a wonderful way to relax quickly. Perhaps we should do it at the end of the day when we get in from work! The second thing that happens is that whatever's at the top of your healing pile comes to the surface, and you start to relive it. In reliving it, you relieve it, ready to be resolved and integrated.

Reliving an issue can bring up deep buried trauma, as with Sarah. Sarah felt irritated by a short conversation with a male colleague – she had felt slighted and harassed, even though neither slight nor harassment had been intended. Whilst receiving ESR, suddenly Sarah broke away, opened her eyes and exclaimed 'I can't, it's too much!' She then tearfully explained that this recent brief incident was reminding her of deep trauma when she had been abused as a teenager by her stepfather. We left ESR for the time being. Sarah took a homeopathic remedy and some flower essences, which supported the resolution of much of the buried issue. Some months later, Sarah could look back on all the incidents, the recent and the past, as resolved, and has used ESR happily on many occasions since.

If you experience a strong emotion when receiving ESR, it's OK to sob, to cry, to scream, or to express the original emotion to catalyse resolution. All these reactions are common, they happen as part of the natural reliving of an issue that was suppressed at the time.

As giver of ESR, allow the process to continue for as long as the receiver wishes. If you sense the receiver's attention drifting off, away from the issue, you may gently guide them back. In fact, the more intensely they can concentrate on the original issue, the quicker it resolves. And then, suddenly the issue will have gone – Relived, Relieved, Experienced, Expressed, Resolved and Integrated.

Then, as giver, it is your responsibility to bring the person back to earth (literally, for they have been away in their imagination). Gently ask them 'When you are ready, in your own time, allow your consciousness, your mind, to return back – back to (the year), to (the date), and (the day of the week). Allow yourself to come back into this (place), this room, and into your body. When you feel comfortable in your body, you may wish to stretch your toes, wriggle your fingers. When you are ready, in your own time, allow your eyes to open'.

Remember, as giver, to make sure the receiver is grounded. You can ask the person to feel their connection with the earth, or more prosaically, the ground pressing up against their feet. If you still suspect the person is ungrounded, you might then wish to check their Chakras, especially the lower and Earth Star (the one below your feet). *Working With Your Chakras* by Ruth White has useful hints. Finally, using Blue Hyacinth Alc flower essence is a powerful grounder if the receiver is still feeling a bit 'spacey'.

Next, as giver, disconnect, give thanks, and cleanse yourself. This may be by washing your hands, it may be by sweeping your aura clear, or it may be doing a quick ESR on yourself to resolve whatever you might have picked up despite the safety belts.

As receiver, allow yourself to settle, and make sure you clap your hands and stamp your feet before driving a car or doing any other task. Also give thanks, and perhaps ponder on the experience.

Now we can all do this for ourselves, as for each other. Done on a regular basis, it makes sure that the washing up is done and the disk defragmented.

ESR is one of the simplest techniques used for blots. We've also heard in Blots, Stains, Tangles and Cobwebs about using flower essences. Let's look at this in a little more detail.

FLOWER ESSENCES

To live life intuitively – in tune with our Selves – isn't always easy. It's not at all difficult to go off track, to go off balance, and to allow imbalances to creep in. Stains can develop, stains which can be resolved by retuning. Essences are an excellent way to resolve stains.

Luckily, in nature we can find many tuning forks to help us rebalance, realign, and release stored patterns of imbalances. Just looking at the sea, or gazing at trees waving in the wind, is deeply soothing. So too is the rustle of leaves, the feel of a gentle breeze on the cheek, the touch of sand between your toes on the beach.

Each of these contains harmonic wave forms. In turn these harmonic wave forms act upon our senses, and our unseen electromagnetic body, to produce harmony, retuning the parts of our consciousness that are out of sync, restoring balance and calm. In turn again, this harmony produces pleasurable feelings, which as we have seen, produce pleasure giving endorphins, our body's natural bliss chemical transmitters.

As we also know, just thinking about the right situation can act as a tuning fork to rebalance us. It's the good vibes we are picking up. We can recapture a pleasurable feeling at will, we can imagine the sea, the sand, the trees, or flowers.

However, we can only imagine things within our library of experience. What is more, imagining something, in order to capture the essence of it, isn't always easy.

This is where flower essences and other vibrational essences can be valuable. Using flower essences is a powerful way to take advantage of Nature's tuning forks. Bach Flower Essences are the best known, but nature doesn't limit her generosity. She provides many, many others. Many makers worldwide now create, or rather co-create with nature, essences from flowers, leaves, and the power of nature in a number of different forms.

Each essence can act as a tuning fork to help rebalance and resolve a particular pattern of vibrational imbalance, an imbalance that invariably shows up as some form of emotional imbalance. The use of these essences is a valuable technique to help us on our journey through life, to help us when we get stuck!

Essences are tuning forks from nature. They provide a note, or a pure harmonious pattern of vibration. Such patterns of vibration can help retune aspects of humans, animals, other energy forms or places that are out of balance.

Essences provide specific patterns of harmony which help resolve corresponding patterns of imbalance.

We may carry many, many frozen patterns of imbalance, some recent, some ancient, some personal, some tribal, some near the surface, and some deeply buried. Some are important and demand, or noticeably influence our conscious functioning, some are less important, or lie deeply and imperceptibly submerged. In total, for a single person, these frozen patterns of imbalance contribute to the many blots, stains, tangles and cobwebs that make up our Shadow of unresolved experiences.

However, we can only consciously resolve these patterns of imbalance one at a time, in sequence. We can visualise them as layers and layers of onion skins, each frozen pattern of imbalance needing resolving in turn (though it may require several essences working together to achieve this). We probably have a number of onions on the go, so to speak, so we can actually process and resolve a number of patterns, at the same time, using a number of tuning forks.

When a tuning fork, or essence, is applied to a human energy form, sometimes the likely effect is known. Sometimes, however, due to the many layers of imbalanced patterns that our Shadow contains, the appropriate use of one essence may highlight the immediate need for others. It seems that the resolution of one imbalance can uncover another, which also needs resolution, but with a different tuning fork. This is why an essence which evokes comfort, harmony and balance in twenty people may feel quite uncomfortable to the twenty-first.

Some people choose their essences solely on the basis of written descriptions, whilst trying to analyse intellectually the nature of the pattern of imbalance. This may work well for a system of essences such as the Bach, where there are only thirty-eight well-defined and different essences from which to choose. All credit to Dr Edward Bach for his ability to choose a system and to define them with such precision, and to all those who have worked with them since and discovered and shared more about them. Working intuitively, however, opens other dimensions and vistas, and is to be recommended. It's also fun!

Here's a story of flower essence use which illustrates the stains we may carry. Many of us carry stains from present or from past. There may also be many layers of imbalances that we are carrying.

Faith came to me stressed with overwork. I suggested Elm, for overwhelm, Walnut for hassle, Hornbeam for a Monday-morning feeling, and Scleranthus for decision-making. Six weeks later she came back, happy but weepy. A completely different state. She said she was 'fine' but clearly was not quite normal. Intuitively I read her as needing Gorse, Mustard, Walnut and Wild Rose, a sadness combination for a time about fifteen years previously. Asking her whether she could relate to this, Faith exclaimed 'Why, of course. My father died when I was sixteen, but for about three years we knew he had cancer and was going to die. This weepy but happy state is how I was for the whole of that time.' Happily, the remedies healed this layer, allowing Faith to feel like herself again.

Sometimes single essences are remarkably effective, either for immediate effect, or over a period. Lynne was anxious. Her daughter was in hospital for an operation, and Lynne had care of her young grandson. She took Red Chestnut, and the effect was visible in seconds. Her anxiety dissolved. Red Chestnut helps all mothers, all therapists, and all nurses and doctors, and all managers. All these people care about outcomes, about the people they look after, but often the care becomes imbalanced into worry as well. Taking Red Chestnut resolves the worry, and enables us to care with compassion, but free from anxiety.

Yvonne dowsed an essence for her husband, and chose a single Chakra essence, that for his throat chakra. Nigel would always bottle things up, not speak about issues, and then, a month down the line, blow a gasket! Taken just a few times daily for one week, Yvonne found the complete change remarkable. Nigel was now himself, and found it easy to speak about issues. 'He had nowhere near as much in his backpack', Yvonne said.

Nowadays there are many thousands of essences available from around the world, some well known with much research on them, some less well known. The skill of many makers has helped produce Combination Essences, which have names like Emergency Essence, Rescue Remedy, Stress Essence, Inner Female Essence, The Universe Handles the Details, Fears, Calm and Clear etc. Combinations are a valuable way to start using essences, as is becoming familiar with a starter range such as the Bach, Masters, Australian Bush or others.

However, the most effective way to use such tuning forks is with the precision that intuitive diagnosis brings, thus giving a direct answer without having to formulate the problem in words, try to look up the answer, hope you are correct, and then give it!

WORKING INTUITIVELY

In dealing with your own Shadow – or other people's – the gift of working intuitively is a valuable skill. This is using intuitive methods such as dowsing, kinesiology (muscle testing), or other methods. Now we all have this gift, whether we just 'know' the answer, or whether we use muscle testing or a pendulum to ask 'yes' or 'no'. When you can do this, it opens up whole areas that otherwise remain hidden to the intellect.

Learning to dowse or finger muscle test is discussed in *Lazy Person's Guide to Emotional Healing, Using Flower Essences Successfully*, pp 58–66 by Andrew Tresidder, in *Dowsing for Health* by Dr Patrick MacManaway, *Elements of Pendulum Dowsing* by Tom Graves, *Spiritual Dowsing* by Sig Lonegrin and in *Anyone Can Dowse for Better Health* by Dr Arthur Bailey.

When you do work intuitively, remember to ask for a balanced combination of essences to help with present issues – but you can also dowse for past issues, for significant dates of trauma, for relationship questions, and a whole host of issues. Do also remember that you can only obtain true answers by dowsing or muscle testing if you have no personal emotional investment in the answer. Otherwise, you will get a true answer that is true only as far as your own bias is concerned – which may start to cause problems.

This is the one major pitfall of working intuitively – if you have any outstanding personal issues, you have to resolve them before you can help someone else, at any but the most basic level. This of course may be the reason why you are drawn to certain circumstances – because your own Higher Self/Intuition sets up a learning experience for you in conjunction with others.

What do we mean by own outstanding personal issues? One day I was trying to be too clever and choose intuitively some essences to help a colleague. He hadn't asked me and was, in fact, rather irritated. I tried to convince him of his need, for an issue of sadness that I identified some fifteen years before in his past. He resisted and denied any problems. I fell into an embarrassed silence when I realised (a) that the fifteen years ago sadness was my issue, not his, and (b) how rude I had been in inflicting unasked for help – it is a classic mistake to try and play Rescuer in life, rather than deal with your own issues. And I was wrong!

On another occasion, I thought that I would choose a set of essences to buy – but found that as I selected each one in turn, I was changing into a more balanced state! By the end of half a dozen, I felt quite different, and my voice and whole demeanour had settled to a calmer state! So, although my conscious intention had been to choose some essences to buy, my deeper needs had specified which essences and chosen me a sequence to rebalance. This sequential processing, healing onion skins in quick sequence, can be a valuable technique.

When we work intuitively (for the highest good of all, of course), e.g. with a pendulum, there are four basic questions that we should start every session with, and if needed, recheck again. They are. . .

'Please show me a Yes',

'Please show me a No',

'Am I fit to dowse?' (i.e. am I in a fit state – do I have my own needs)

'May I talk about. . .?' (i.e. permission)

I suspect in the case mentioned above I was not fit to dowse – and I certainly didn't have permission!

Even if you are working as a therapist and have considerable skill with our tools, if your tools (for instance flower essences) are needed by you, you will automatically (intuitively) choose essences for your own needs, even if your will is trying to override this.

HOMEOPATHY

Homeopathy is the use of the energy imprint of substances to stimulate the life force into healing a corresponding pattern of imbalance – a bit like the bulbous bow on a supertanker which aims to cancel out the waveform produced, thus making the ship more economical to run. Substances are used in minute doses, so it cannot be any physical substance causing an effect.

Homeopathy is well known for healing emotional problems, as well as physical ones. Often, there are several layers of emotional imbalance, so one remedy will need to be followed by another. Mary had two bereavements in quick succession. Ignatia in repeated doses helped her with the short-term grief that kept bubbling up to the surface, whilst Natrum Mur was able to help unfreeze a tighter pattern of frozen emotion, and allow her tears to flow.

Caution note – if you feel depressed, especially if you feel worthlessness or guilt, or suicidal, do please seek medical attention urgently – it helps to share the burden, and the professional is there to help. They may be able to prescribe antidepressants or advise on another course of action. Also, bereavement can be a time of strong emotions and vulnerability, so do seek professional help to help you understand and work through the process of grieving. And if you become depressed, do seek medical help.

Some cases of homeopathic use for emotional imbalance have amazed me. Jack seemed to need several of the 'sadness' flower essences for his deep despair but, for whatever reason, chose to take Aurum Met (homeopathic gold). Over six days his depression lifted, and he returned to his normal self, without using the flower essences, or the prescribed antidepressant.

Ruth was a sensitive person and had been hit hard by grief. It had caused a deep resentment to smoulder inside her. Staphisagria brought about a resolution over a few days. She could no longer feel the resentment.

Charlotte fell ill on holiday due to overheating. Sulphur changed her briefly back to normal, but uncovered a layer of quite malevolent flashes of temper. It took me a few days to find the right remedy, one of the miasmatic remedies, Medorrhinum. At which point, she changed, dramatically, and very much for the better.

REGRESSION

We all use regression when we look back at old memories. It has been developed into a therapeutic technique to help people in very specific ways.

Regression is a technique that helps people look for the original traumas that affect them. There are several ways to do it, one of the simplest being guided visualisation. However, when the trauma surfaces, it may be painful and, as in Diana's case, provoke a brief worsening of her asthma, as the original trauma was relived. Diana had at this point used flower essences for several months, with the effect of resolving much sadness that had stuck with her from life's events in her adult years.

'Ever since I can remember, I have always been afraid of small spaces and enclosed areas – claustrophobia. I don't like cupboards, attics, small rooms, caves, or locked doors. Even cars can be a problem I am aware that this fear is irrational, but it is a very strong feeling. I overcome it in the main by avoiding all these situations, and I now realise by, of course, suppressing the fear. The older I am, the stronger the fear seems to get.

'In these situations I am always looking for an escape route. In a hotel I will always ask for a ground floor room, whilst I avoid lifts like the plague! I never get into one alone, and would rather use the stairs!

'Regression brought this very much to light and out into the open. During a session we were asked to imagine ourselves walking down a long, dark, narrow tunnel with a closed door at the end. I soon began to be afraid, to sweat, shiver and gasp for breath – I started to develop the beginnings of one of my asthma attacks. After using my inhaler, I gradually calmed down. Early the next morning I awoke terrified from a nightmare, in which I had been shut in a small place in the dark. In time I was able to calm myself down, and after using my inhaler, the original cause of all my fears came flooding back. When I was four-and-a-half, my three-year-old brother locked me in the cupboard under the stairs. From what I have been told since, my fears all started at this time. It was a difficult time for the family, as my mother was dying from tuberculosis, and we children were left very much to our own devices. My asthma started at this point. I am sure it was compounded by the blocked emotion of missing a mother's love for her children all through my life, especially as my brother was killed in a rail accident at the young age of thirty-two.'

Since this regression, and taking flower essences, Diana has steadily felt better in herself, and coincidentally her asthma has been less troublesome.

KEEPING CLEANSING

The key point about Keep Cleansing, Stay Grounded is to keep doing the washing up (of your unresolved emotions) and keep spring-cleaning the house (of your non-physical body)!

If the washing up isn't done, you get piles and piles of dirty cups and plates, whilst if the spring-cleaning isn't done, you end up with cobwebs, dust and musty smells everywhere.

We've looked at a few simple tools we can use on Blots and Stains – but the ones we've looked at here are by no means the only ones to use – the main thing is to find the tools that work for each of us.

So let's just recap on how to carry on washing up and spring-cleaning. First, as we've seen, is getting started. Melt or thaw the denial that freezes our response. Next, bring it up to the light of day, throw open the windows, let a breath of fresh air blow through.

Communication, Expression and Reflection are the vital points.

Denial freezes Communication.

Denial freezes Expression.

Denial freezes Reflection.

Thawing the denial mechanism allows us to start communicating again, both with ourselves, within, and with others outside. Effective communication demands Alignment, Balance and Connection. If you make space, Reflection automatically follows. This applies to *all* our issues.

Remember the map. If Expression is blocked, we collect unresolved issues – frozen patterns of imbalance. So Communication (if only to ourselves), Expression and Reflection facilitate resolution of the unfinished washing up (as well as dealing with today's work today).

Ways of Expressing ourselves can be through use of our body (dance and movement), our voice (singing, humming, chanting, talking), our words (poetry, writing a letter), our thoughts (getting in touch with, or sending, thoughts out) and even through our breathing (transformational breathing).

Expression can be gentle, such as a quiet conversation and honest communication of feelings in normal tones, or it can be like a thunderclap, such as a tantrum! The energy released can be channelled constructively or destructively. As we saw in Chapter Two, in fact, any build-up of emotional charge can be cleared by a rapid discharge, such as a flash of anger, a flush of ecstasy, a rush of creativity, a burst of laughter, or a flood of tears. Each is cathartic in its way, clearing away the intensely felt emotion in a rapid flow of release. In fact, it is nigh on impossible to keep feeling an intensity of emotion without provoking a powerful Expression, leading to Resolution – it is when we block the flow of an emotion that we prevent a Release from happening. Creative expression deliberately using the emotions is how musicians, artists, writers, poets, dancers and others actually work, using the map of the emotions constructively.

Emotional Expression
can be either
Constructive
or
Destructive

Expression can involve an uplifting outlook, to help oneself and others – a stance of Forgiveness – or it can seek to steal energy from others – Criticism. This reflects both our personal stance – and society's – whether, for instance, we feel unsupported and living in a Blame culture, or whether we feel supported and are able to sustain an Appreciation Culture.

Curiously, we can switch from one to the other, from the uplifting to the energy-stealing, from the positive to the negative, in a flash – and also vice-versa! The switch from negative to positive is not so easy, but can be facilitated by a positive tuning fork to rebalance us, such as humour, or a tuning fork from nature such as a flower essence. Both aid Inner Communication, healthy Expression and thus a Reflective Resolution.

Techniques we can use include:

* Meditation
* Forgiveness
* Writing a letter (even if we don't send it)
* Talking an issue through
* Life Coaching skills

* Journey Therapy (initiated by Brandon Bays and described in her book *The Journey*) is a powerful way to get in touch with our inner being, which helps us transcend and see beyond any unresolved issues)
* Breathing, particularly transformational breathing
* Flower essence use
* Shamanistic journeying
* Instant Emotional Healing – acupressure for the emotions, as elaborated by Peter Lambrou and George Pratt
* Neuro-Linguistic Programming (NLP) – a system of re-framing our thoughts and therefore our emotions

Some of these techniques have not been covered in this book. Please use the resource section to continue on your healing journey.

And don't forget to ask for Help. We all think we're alone, but there are other people around us, as well as realms of invisible helpers just waiting. According to many cultures we each have a Guardian Angel available at all times. True or not, if you believe it, it becomes true! So even if you're not a gambler, you may like to hedge your bets!

DEALING WITH TANGLES

Tangles, to recap, involve unresolved emotional issues between two (or more) individuals. Allowing the tangles to persist means we allow ourselves to be chained by past issues, by past relationships. To dissolve a tangle requires bringing the issue up to the surface. Then it can be:

* Accepted
* Acknowledged

* Forgiven
* Released

and we are free to Move On.

Bringing the warmth of a loving supported reflection to an issue can do this. A Forgiveness meditation is a particularly powerful tool, as can be visualisation, and a cutting or a melting (with love) of the ties that bind. Sometimes a tuning fork such as a flower essence can also resolve a tangle. Guided meditation is another helpful technique, as can be an emotional stress resolution hold.

Reflection is important. We've all had times when we felt frustrated with someone else, even if that emotion was a projected one, not just caused by the person themselves. Other people can easily become the scapegoat for our own unresolved issues. When, later, we talk the issue through with someone else (tell the story) we can reflect upon it whilst they offer us their empathy and support. So, find a friend who can listen and support you whilst you express your feelings.

Writing a letter, especially if you don't send it, can be a powerful way of resolving a tangle. How often have we wished we could say things to someone, but either let the opportunity slip by, or were too afraid or worried to give voice to our thoughts.

The letter can be burnt or torn up if you wish, often it's better than sending it! Just the written expression of our emotions can catalyse a resolution of the tangle.

One tangle was caused by three business friends failing to express their feelings. As a result of work and other external pressures on each of them, they all became tired and emotionally drained. Two compensated by retreating into numb mechanical silence, the other over-compensated by excessive enthusiasm. The two felt dominated, but failed to say anything. Sarah had many home worries, and small children. Jane had recently lost her mother, and was grieving for her and other emotional issues had come up for her. Sarah and Jane retreated into silence and stopped communicating with Fiona. Fiona was also tired, but her compensation was an addiction to adrenaline. She acted this out by coming up with grand projects, working fast and hard, and she failed to notice that her two friends were no longer communicating with her. The result was that one of the friends became ill, and blamed the others for the problem. Happily, the three were able to talk things through before the situation became too fraught. Issues were resolved, things that had been taken for granted were acknowledged, the illness resolved, and balance returned to three wiser friends. After all, it had only been a logjam of business and personal pressures, and a failure to allow time for Communication, Expression and Reflection, that had caused the problem in the first place.

The following letter might well be written in many different circumstances (even if never sent) to help in expressing and resolving issues.

Dear Friend

Thank you for your patience whilst I expressed my feelings, and for all you do, and for helping me understand this:

The world is moving (one hopes) from a Blame Culture to an Appreciation Culture. One of the problems we all have as human beings is an inability to express our feelings honestly, without denying them, and without projecting them at someone else (or ourselves). Our feelings, after all, are our feelings, irrespective of the original (or many) sources of these feelings.

If they are indeed our feelings, then we have to own them, take responsibility for them, and resolve them ourselves. And perhaps it's important that in society we each acknowledge our differences, and also give ourselves (and each other) time to deal with issues that come up – otherwise unresolved issues build up into a logjam of major feelings. So let us try to understand one another and help each other to resolve any issues that could come between us.

Thanks for reading this

Your Friend

Forgiveness Meditation

A Forgiveness Meditation is a very powerful way to resolve a personal tangle. First allow yourself to sit comfortably. When ready, remember that we are all part of all things, and all related to one another. Next, imagine a safe place, such as a garden, or your favourite chair. Feel relaxed and supported by the familiarity, the peace, and the beauty of the place.

Walking from afar, you recognise coming closer the person whom you dislike, or feel anger toward, or hurt by. The person, or people come slowly towards you. In your mind's eye, allow yourself to rise, and offer a symbol of love, peace and forgiveness. This may be a smile, an open hand, or a warm outpouring of love. Notice how the other person feels, and be aware of your own feelings. Be Aligned to the situation. Keep Balanced. Maintain Connection with the feeling of support. Allow yourself to make eye contact with the other person. Allow warm, healing energy to flow from your heart, and your whole body to the other person. They may look away. Allow them, in their own time, to look at you again. When you have eye contact again, allow love to flow. 'I'm sorry' may be appropriate. When finished, allow the other person to be free. Salute them as a fellow traveller in life, and as your teacher (we are all here to teach each other, and it's often the ones who love us the most on one level who give us the hardest time, and the most opportunity for growth!).

Give thanks. Reflect.

Come back to the present. Feel your mind come back into your body, into the present day. Stretch your toes, wiggle your fingers, and allow your eyes to gently open. Allow yourself to congratulate yourself. Well done! Have compassion, not just for others but for yourself too.

You can use a forgiveness meditation at any time, for anyone else, and to forgive yourself too. We've all given ourselves a hard time more than once. We all beat ourselves up about something or other, so why not forgive yourself, too. You can also say sorry to your physical body, if you've ever had an injury, or an operation, or any form of hurt.

Tangles can come from other times and other places. Jan had always had a difficult relationship with her mother. She could never do anything right. Her father had died when she was three. Now thirty, she still felt antipathy toward her mother, although her mother was now in her sixties, and ill with cancer. Jan asked a friend to 'hold the space for her', as she felt an unhealed issue coming close to the surface. The friend held her forehead and back in the emotional stress release hold.

Jan, gifted with intuition, found herself transported back, in her imagination, to a seventeenth-century village. She was a sixteen-year-old girl in a hovel. Her mother there was an older woman. A man appeared, the woman's husband. He chose to pay attention to Jan, the girl. The woman became inwardly bitter, though she said nothing. As Jan described this, tears flowed. The relationship flourished, the older woman's bitterness grew. The end of the seventeenth-century story was not happy, and reliving the tragic outcome brought floods of tears to Jan.

It was obvious that this visualisation was connecting Jan to some deep emotions within her, even if the story was only in her imagination. With her friend 'holding the space', Jan was able to resolve her emotions, and offer forgiveness to the situation. When she opened her eyes, she said 'Mother' and realised she now felt quite differently toward her mother, who was ill with cancer. She now had a maturity of compassion that she could honestly feel – rather than know it was how she ought to feel.

We each have 'karmic' tangles (unresolved issues) with many of the key players in our lives. These may involve personal issues of violence and violation, of death and murder, of hurt and hurt feelings. Yet each can be resolved in turn, leaving us lighter and freer, and often happier in this lifetime. More spring-cleaning done!

One final technique on resolving tangles is to see yourself and the other person connected by a thread or rope, which entwines the two of you in a figure of eight. You can see that this puts each of you in a circle, the two circles held together. You can imagine the emotional ties, the fear, the anger, the pain, or the guilt that tie these two circles together, and hold them bound up with one another. If you can imagine these ties existing, you can also imagine them dissolving! So now imagine them dissolving, with the gentle warmth of love, of the sequence of Accept, Acknowledge, Forgive, Release and Move On.

Now you can see the two circles (the two people) separate. The ties are melted, the bonds dissolved. You are both now free, and forgiven!

Something that can happen in a relationship is that we can lose a bit of ourself to another person – in shaman's terms, we lose a bit of our soul. We can also have bits of our soul fragmented by trauma. A shaman will journey on behalf of a client to reclaim and restore the lost part of the soul.

Bob had used shamanic techniques since his teens. When his father died, Bob felt that a part of his own soul had fragmented. He used drumming to enable himself to meet his spirit guide, a native American, who took him to his father, who then proceeded to explain to Bob the workings of the spirit realm. Bob found this amusing, not least because in his lifetime, his father had always been a complete sceptic about Bob's interest, and had made fun of him. (Guides, by the way, are often from cultures with native wisdom about the invisible worlds, such as Aboriginals, Native Americans, Druids or others.)

DESIRES AND URGES

The two most basic desires and urges we possess are primeval ones of survival and procreation. Desires and urges are mentioned here because they certainly seem to be able to get us into tangles!

These drives can be so powerful in animals as to completely dominate their behaviour – survival when cornered or sex when in season. Anyone who has ever had a dog as a pet will know exactly what we mean.

Knowing ourselves means being aware of our drives and urges, and channelling them responsibly (if you possibly can). Certainly, being aware helps. Many sensible mothers describe to their teenage daughters both the romance of love, and the caveat that young men can have particularly strong drives and urges. Young men (and women) however, are not always adept at overriding basic biological urges. This subject is rather bigger than this book – so we'll leave it here, except to say:

Beware feeding the urges excessively

Beware becoming addicted to urges

Beware the phenomenal strength of hormonal drives and instincts, whether resulting from oestrogen, testosterone, or the basic toning hormone in the body, thyroxine. Overactive or underactive urges of these hormones can be a challenge to manage, and require balance, careful managing and appropriate resolution on all levels.

Finally, beware that you're not being driven by a cobweb such as an archetype of the Seven Deadly Sins.

DEALING WITH COBWEBS

In What's in My Shadow, Blots & Stains, Tangles & Cobwebs, we saw the story of Rhona, whose aunt had died, but was still earthbound to the house where Rhona lived. We saw that the aunt moved to the light when encouraged to do so.

As well as stuck souls, cobwebs include all sorts of thought forms and psychic junk, thought forms that circle the world.

At times, we can be vulnerable to invasion by these thought forms, and sometimes we contain them already. What do we mean by this? Well, archetypally, we all carry patterns that allow in fear, the Seven Deadly Sins (Pride, Wrath, Envy, Lust, Gluttony, Avarice and Sloth). In the ether of the world there's not only thousands of radio and TV channels, but also all the thought forms of humanity. These include whole hosts of negative thought forms, fears, worries, anxieties, and so on. They can be given names, such as Spirit of Fear, Spirit of Cancer, Spirit of Frustration and hundreds of others.

When our physical health is low, we are susceptible to illness. We can catch cold and end up with a virus or other sickness.

In the same way, if our energetic health is low, we are susceptible to taking on patterns of imbalance such as cobwebs. In fact, if we are out of balance, out of harmony, we can attract and maintain imbalances. These can include various negative thought forms, both personal and generic. But, if we can let a pattern in, we can also release it!

All patterns of imbalance can be re-tuned and re-harmonised, or they can be drowned out by a stronger vibration.

Evangelical deliverance is one form of using an extremely powerful vibration, that of alignment to God and Christ, to push out negative thought forms. One-third of Jesus' Ministry in the New Testament was deliverance (casting out of demons), the other two-thirds, teaching and healing. Jesus cautioned of the pitfalls of deliverance – firstly, casting out one may let in seven more – i.e. a person may have a susceptible pattern, so not only do you need deliverance, but also to strengthen your energy patterns, or aura, to prevent the same happening again. Second, was the problem of where the spirits (demons) would go. One group asked to be allowed into some pigs, which promptly charged off the cliff and drowned themselves.

Certainly, in a spirit of love, rather than confrontation, we would wish such imbalances to be re-patterned and re-harmonised. After all, what you resist, persists, so perhaps we should aim to raise our vibes using prayer, meditation, cleansing, and tuning forks such as essences in order to minimise and dissolve our susceptibilities (and avoid all the situations that make us susceptible). And should there be any negative entities or patterns remaining, we may ask them firmly to return to where they belong, and cease troubling those with whom they have no business. *ET101* by Mission Control has some useful hints on this!

In a way, resolving cobwebs is Alignment, Balance, and Connection in action, albeit on very unseen levels.

Cobwebs are a huge area where spirituality and physical reality intermix, traditionally the preserve of the priest, religion or secret practices. This whole area is ripe for investigation over the next few years, as mankind seeks to heal our invisible wounds and imbalances. Sorry, we haven't got all the answers yet, but let's work on it together!

CHAPTER 7

Healing People, Healing Places

'Our emotions must not be clouded, for our true self cannot shine clearly through muddied water.'

Jane Bertram

We live in a very exciting time for humanity. The opportunities for growth are immense, although the challenges for each of us, and for governments, can also be huge.

Broadly speaking, over the last thousand years, we have gained great experience and expertise in our culture. Much of the world has adequate food, shelter, clothing and warmth. We have moved on from illiteracy. We've had the Agricultural Revolution and the Transport Revolution (several times, with the advent of canals, railways, cars, and air travel). Communication has been revolutionised – the information technology revolution has changed the world.

Power has been globalised – yet also individualised, so we can each now take our power and use it as we wish.

Freed from much of the struggle to make the physical world work to our advantage, we now have the challenge of dominating and subjugating the invisible Emotional World.

Or do we? Perhaps the opportunity is to be more gentle with ourselves and others, to learn the maps of emotion, to heal ourselves and to do our spring-cleaning on our Blots, Stains,

Tangles and Cobwebs, to learn skills of how to make the best of life's journey in a physical body, unencumbered by invisible Shadows?

In making ourselves better, we automatically change the world by changing ourselves, and we enable ourselves and our civilisation to use the opportunities for growth to best advantage. Well, at least it's better than being pushed off your bicycle!

As we heal ourselves we become aware of the energies of places, how they can feel good, or how they can carry negative imprints of disharmony

Much of the disharmony is due to human beings – or rather due to the emotional incontinence of human beings who spray or drop negative emotions widely. But if we can sense emotions in places, we can also heal them, using visualisation, our own energies, or other healing energies. Energy follows thought, so a focused Intention can be a powerful force for the good if you wish!

And if we have a strong Intention to heal a place, it will happen. Just as we can hold within us unresolved patterns of imbalance as Blots, Stains, Tangles and Cobwebs, so places can also hold unresolved patterns, in similar Blots, Stains, Tangles and Cobwebs.

In healing a place, if we bring an issue (an unresolved pattern of imbalance) to mind, we can help it Express and Resolve – it can be Accepted, Acknowledged, Forgiven, Released and Moved On.

We may need to use any or all of the healing techniques we've discussed through the book, and possibly some others besides, adapting them as the situation demands.

As we work to clean ourselves and our inner imbalances, and bring harmony, automatically the outer physical world will improve. Our landscapes and cities can be filled with beauty and balance, or haunted by ugliness and imbalance, whichever we choose. (Of course, nature has just a bit of a hand in it, too!) Working to clear imbalances, and working in harmony with the natural energies of the world, using Feng Shui and other sciences, changes everything towards harmony and balance.

Then, we can live and work with inner harmony and balance, and manifest outer harmony and balance, to reflect that which is within. With clear balanced emotions, our true selves can shine through for mutual benefit.

As we change ourselves, we help to change the world, even if only slightly. After all, quantum physics tells us that a distant planet is affected by the beat of a butterfly's wings – or, (as read with the typo uncorrected) a distant planet is affected by a butterfly breaking wind! Take your pick – as far as quantum physics is concerned, they're both true!

And as we become whole ourselves, we find it easier to relate to the beauty of nature, to honour it, and to help maintain and create beauty in the world.

The challenge is to stay balanced, and deal with what comes up, as it appears, rather than leaving all the cleaning for another day, or another year!

SPACE CLEARING

One of the problems is that human beings are emotionally incontinent, or at least most of us aren't yet potty trained, so we drop emotions and feelings all over the place!

This was brought home to me on holiday in Cornwall. The cliff walk to the newsagent was delightful, but fifty yards from the shop, I started to feel most uncomfortable. This feeling intensified into a strong knowing that something was badly wrong as I walked toward the entrance. And, there on the news stand, was every national daily, an orange picture of Concorde on fire in the sky covering the front page. What I had picked up was the shock, horror and fear that had been dropped by every reader over the past hour since the shop had opened. A case for Emergency Essence 30c, Five Flower 30c or some other powerful space clearing vibration. These vibrations can be used either as the homeopathic tablet to clear a space as well as the more usual blessing with white light. It seems that homeopathic potentisation can give a more powerful energy to help clear spaces of trauma. This is particularly useful for battlefields, sites of murder or other trauma, or major disruption to earth energy lines. However, this is a subject for a book in itself!

Before a recent gathering, I was privileged to watch two masters of the art of space clearing.

The Conference Centre was regularly used for management training, and for intense studious learning. I hadn't appreciated that the vibes of the place might not be ideal, but when Steve pointed it out, it was obvious. Before the gathering began, Steve and Jane took care to clean the room that we'd all be listening to the lectures in. The energy in the room was not unhappy or offensive, as it can be at times, and there was no obvious psychic presence or entity, or heavy vibes of fear or terror, such as you may find at the site of a murder or traumatic event. What there appeared to be was a sensation of intense mental concentration, perhaps a little joyless and sombre.

Steve and Jane's tools were smudging sticks, Tibetan healing bowls and a bell, and three combination sprays from the Alaskan Range. In order of use, these were Purification, to clear the space of unwanted energies, Guardian, which protects the clear space, and Calling All Angels, which invokes and brings in a wonderful feeling into any space. These sprays of course contain flower, gem and environmental essences, and some aromatherapy oils. A few minutes of dedicated careful clearing left the lecture hall feeling lighter and vibrant, ideal conditions for the next five days of flower essence presentations.

If we don't clear a space before using it, whether hotel room, lecture hall, bedroom, living space, new home or plane or train seat, then inevitably we may allow ourselves to pick up unwanted vibes which can lower our own energy levels. And, of course, if we don't clear our own space after using it, it's rather like not washing up or making the bed, or not clearing up your workplace.

Sometimes you have to use a few other techniques in your space clearing – and in clearing your own space. This story may be of interest:

The sun was shining but the house felt heavy inside and though the police service had thoroughly cleaned and tidied away all traces of blood and trauma there was a palpable stain of fear and terror in the house. I suspected this came from both the dead man's last moments at home, whilst desperately ill, and from James' horror and shock at the sight he had found. The three Alaskan sprays cleared this heaviness, together with the calling in of Rescue 30c (I didn't have any with me). Then, it felt as though the friend was still earth bound, as many souls are when their passing has been sudden or traumatic. A few simple words helped move the soul on into the light.

If you haven't already read *Dead Happy* by Lance Trendall, do try and find time to – everyone involved in any form of healing will at some time find they are in contact with a stuck soul or entity. And sometimes the stuck soul decides to stick to you – as I've found at least twice with patients of mine who have passed on. The key is to remember and affirm your own space, and to gently ask that soul to look for the light and move towards it, perhaps helped by some loved ones. It is important to use the Lord's Prayer, and whatever protection of your own space you may have learnt. Even vicars and doctors can get caught out occasionally – but that's another story!

Space clearing is an important skill that has many facets. To help us, we can use healing vibrations, such as sound, colour, light, sprays and nature's other gifts. They are tools to help us, no different to using tools and gadgets in our house cleaning and washing up. Imagine washing up greasy plates without detergent. Yuk! Flower essence sprays are particularly powerful tools to help us clear spaces – the vibrational equivalent of air freshener!

If flower essences, sound and light are powerful space clearers, then how much more powerful is Mother Nature herself? Nature's glories are always uplifting, whether they be landscapes, mountains, fields, or gardens – and, as we have seen, full of powerful tuning forks to bring about harmony and balance.

May we finish our journey together with the following stories?

ABC in an Emergency

Let's look at how we can help ourselves with an emergency. These were Kate's experiences.

Kate had been married twice but found security in her new partner. When he left, she was devastated. In shock, she was too paralysed by fear to be able to think how to help herself. She had lost A B and C – alignment, balance and connection.

Fortunately, a friend was able to remind her of what she had forgotten – to regain A B and C. Kate slowed down her breathing to reconnect. She had a set of flower remedies, but felt too out of balance to choose for herself. Emergency Essence helped her a little, but she was too numbed to remember to take it regularly. However, sitting with the remedies, she placed her hand over them, and was drawn first to Cerato, to restore connection to our inner voice. She held the bottle, and felt calmer. After a minute, she next chose Rock Rose, for courage at times of terror. Holding it again calmed her. Impatiens came next, for irritability, then Centaury, for affirming our boundaries, followed by Walnut, to protect us against other people's emotions.

Kate felt stiller and calmer – and then a wave of emotion rose up and overwhelmed her again – this had all happened before in her life. She felt anguish, upset, sadness, anger – a whole mixture of emotions. Her friend reminded her to keep breathing slowly, and to practice ESR. So Kate placed her hand on her forehead, breathed slowly, and felt the wave of emotion resolve.

She now noticed that, though she was no longer shaking, her hands were cold, and her feet tingly. Had we been able to study her aura, we would have seen stuck energy at her extremities, building up, not being released. Kate remembered to connect to the earth, as well as to upstairs, and asked out loud for the emotion to be returned to Mother Earth for cleansing and recycling. Almost immediately, her hands and feet returned to normal.

Ten minutes after starting to help herself, Kate was back in Alignment, Balance, and Connection. She felt better, and now had things in perspective again.

MEANING IN LIFE

Our lives are perhaps a journey of experiences, whose purpose is a quest for meaning. We each express this in different ways, each to be true to our personal individual selves as part of that journey. And if we are called by our intuition to do something *now*, then we do well to act on the instant.

Trisha, a midwife, was late leaving for work, and her partner reminded her to take out the rubbish. He became irritated when Trisha told him that she just had to write a poem. 'A poem, for goodness sake!' he exclaimed. Now poetry came to Trisha infrequently, but always had poignant meaning when it did – so she knew she just had to capture the thoughts in her mind, and commit them to paper. The poems always had meaning for her, and related to recent incidents in her life. This was the result. As Trisha put it, 'This is the story of a young woman. I was her midwife and cared for her during her pregnancy, labour and in the days following the birth. I witnessed her anguish and pain, as she did what she believed was the right thing to do. I was overwhelmed by her courage and wrote the following poem . . . I never shared it with her, perhaps I will one day.'

My Gift by Adoption

No longer joined by umbilical cord
This baby of mine was taken;
To the waiting arms of a barren soul
Leaving me so empty and shaken.
My arms are lacking what they hold so dear
And my heart feels truly broken.
I wished for so much, now the future I fear –
All I have is a photo – a token.
How can this baby, who physically has gone,
Still be joined to me by a cord so long?
That wrenches so hard on my heart and mind,
While I'm isolated by others so blind
Who have no concept of what has occurred
And only gossip about what they have heard
But yet have no wish to communicate with me
On a subject, so complex, they really can't see.

So I forge on the wiser, and superior too
For in my short life I have done more than you.
Trisha Bailey

The story behind the poem was this: A young woman attended college to achieve the requisite qualifications for university. A relationship that meant everything to her resulted in an unplanned pregnancy. The father of her unborn child was in love with the young woman, however his parents advised him that to 'tie himself down' and pledge commitment to a young woman and this unborn child would be detrimental to his future. His loyalty to his parents outweighed his love for the young woman.

Alone and unsupported, abandoned in love and facing uncertainty, the young woman chose to honour the life growing within her. She considered her options of keeping her baby or giving the child up for adoption. One morning, near the end of her pregnancy, she came downstairs to see two envelopes on the doormat. One contained a letter offering her a long sought-after place at Oxford University, the other contained adoption papers.

She held the letters, one in each hand, looking from one to the other, the decision made all the more poignant by them arriving on the same day. She chose to give her baby the love of both a mother and father. She gave adoptive parents the most precious gift on earth . . . a child to love. She went to university.

In life, we have many choices and challenges. And every single one is a chance for growth. What an opportunity life is!

HEALING PEOPLE, HEALING PLACES

Healing places as well as ourselves is a pretty tall order – but it can be fun? Many people now use Feng-Shui and space clearing techniques. To look at the bigger picture as to how to heal places, you might like to take tips from people who've got some experience. Try www.fountain-international.org or www.zoence.com for some tips and inspiration!

Thank you for joining me in learning to unblock our emotions – and if you've made it this far in the book – well done!

Together we can work to heal ourselves and each other, and in doing so, help make the world a better place. May I please offer you a Native American prayer to help us come to a close:

Grandfather, Look At Our Brokenness

Grandfather,
Look at our brokenness.

We know that in all creation
Only the human family
Has strayed from the sacred way.

We know that we are the ones
Who are divided
And we are the ones
Who must come back together
To walk in the sacred way.

Grandfather,
Sacred one,

Teach us love, compassion and honour
That we may heal the earth
And heal each other.

Good luck!

Resources

Adrienne, Carol, *The Purpose of Your Life*

Alexander, Jane, *Mind, Body and Spirit*

Ashworth, David, *Dancing with the Devil (As You Channel in the Light)*

Bach, Dr Edward, *Heal Thyself*

Bailey, Dr Arthur, *Anyone Can Dowse for Better Health*

Barefoot Doctor's Guide for the Urban Warrior

Barnard, Julian, *Patterns of Life Force*

Bays, Brandon, *The Journey*

Berne, Eric, *Games People Play*

Berne, Eric, *I'm OK, You're OK*

Bloom, Dr William, *The Endorphin Effect*

Briffa, Dr John, *Ultimate Health*

Butler, Gillian and Hope, Tony, *Manage Your Mind*

Caddy, Eileen, *Opening Doors Within*

Carter-Scott, Dr Cherie, *If Life is a Game, These are the Rules*

Coelho, Paul, *The Alchemist*

Cousins, David, *Handbook for Light Workers*

Cowan, David and Girdlestone, Rodney, *Safe as Houses*

Cooper, Diana, *Transform Your Life*

Covey, Dr Steven, *The Seven Habits of Highly Effective People*

Dawkins, Peter, *Zoence – the Science of Life*

Dethlefsen, Thorwald and Dahlke, Rüdiger, *Healing Powers of Illness*

Dunn, Dr Joseph, *Lazy Person's Guide to Midlife*

Eden, Donna, *Energy Medicine*

Emoto, Masuru, *The Message from Water*

Forward, Dr Susan and Frazier, Donna, *Emotional Blackmail*

Gerber, Dr Richard, *Vibrational Medicine*

Gerber, Dr Richard, *Vibrational Medicine for the 21st Century*

Gimbel, Theo, *Healing with Colour*

Goleman, Dr Daniel, *Emotional Intelligence*

Goleman, Dr Daniel, *Working with Emotional Excellence*

Gray, Dr John, *Men are From Mars, Women from Venus*

Graves, Tom, *Elements of Pendulum Dowsing*

Guirdham, Dr Arthur, *The Psyche in Medicine*

Guirdham, Dr Arthur, *The Psychic Dimensions of Mental Health*

Guirdham, Dr Arthur, *Paradise Found*

Hall, Alan, Water, *Electricity and Health*

Harrold, Fiona, *Be Your Own Life Coach*

Hay, Louise, *You Can Heal Your Life*

Holbeche, Soozi, *Changes*

Humphreys, Dr Peter and Pratt, Dr George, *Instant Emotional Healing*

Humphreys, Tony, *Work and Worth*

Lambillion, Paul, *Auras and Colours, A Guide to Working with Subtle Energies*

Lambillion, Paul, *How to Heal and Be Healed*

Lambrou, Peter and Pratt, George, *Instant Emotional Healing*

Lazaris, George, *Working with the Shadow*

The Lazaris Material, Concept Synergy, P.O. Box 3285, Palm Beach, Florida

Lindenfield, Gael, *Self Esteem*

Lindenfield, Gael, *Managing Anger*

Lonegrin, Sig, *Spiritual Dowsing*

MacManaway, Dr Patrick, *Dowsing for Health*

McGraw, Dr Phillip, *Life Strategies*

McTaggart, Lynne, *The Field*

Miller, Hamish and Broadhurst, Paul, *The Sun and the Serpent*

Miller, Hamish, *It's Not Too Late*

Millman, Dan, *Everyday Enlightenment*

Mission Control, *ET101*

Myss, Dr Caroline, *Anatomy of the Spirit*

Myss, Dr Caroline, *Why People Don't Heal and How They Can*

Ornish, Dr Dean, *Love and Survival*

Page, Dr Christine, *Frontiers of Health*

Page, Dr Christine Page, *The Mind Body Spirit Workbook*

Page, Dr Christine, *The Mirror of Existence*

Pease, Barbara and Alan, *Why Men Don't Listen and Women Can't Read Maps*

Penny, Jannet Unite, *The South African Flower Essences*

Pert, Dr Candace, *Molecules of Emotion*

Prince, Derek, *They Shall Expel Demons*

Redfield, James, *The Celestine Prophecy, a Pocket Guide*

Roberts, Monty, *Horse Sense for People*

Shine, Betty, *The Infinite Mind*

Soskin, Julie, *Insight and Intuition*

Thurnell-Read, Jane, *Geopathic Stress*

Trendall, Lance, *Dead Happy*

Tresidder, Dr Andrew, *Lazy Person's Guide to Emotional Healing, Using Flower Essences Successfully*

Yellowlees, Dr Walter, *A Doctor in the Wilderness*

Wilde, Stuart, *The Force*

Wilde, Stuart, *Infinite Self*

Wilde, Stuart, *Sixth Sense*

Wilde, Stuart, *Affirmations*

Williamson, Vivien, *Bach Remedies and Other Flower Essences*

White, Ruth, *Working With Your Chakras*

Jannet Unite Penny's website is *www.saffloweressences.com*

Healing Places – please visit *www.fountain-international.org*

Andrew's Website *www.dr-andrew-flowers.co.uk*

INDEX

THE LAZY PERSON'S GUIDE TO EMOTIONAL HEALING
Using Flower Essences Successfully

Dr Andrew Tresidder

A refreshing and original text, *Lazy Person's Guide to Emotional Healing* reveals flower essences as power catalysts in transforming negative emotions into positive. By matching the essence appropriate to the emotion that is out of balance, a transformation can occur – often surprisingly swiftly.

In 1930 Dr Edward Bach, the father of modern flower remedy therapy, advanced the theory that emotional, mental and spiritual imbalances can cause disease. Andrew Tresidder brings Bach up to date, explaining the theory underlying flower essences and how they work. He gives numerous examples from his own experience of using flower essences as a general medical practitioner.

Lazy Person's Guide to Emotional Healing includes a flower essence compendium, with 90 remedies commonly found and used. A further 130 combination remedies chosen from major flower essence systems world-wide are analysed and evaluated.

Dr Tresidder's enlightening approach to healing will inspire health professionals as well as those who are open to transforming themselves as catalysts for change.

'One of my favourite books on using flower essences for healing.'

Susan Clark, *The Sunday Times*

'...refreshing and original, an enlightened approach to healing that will inspire you.'

Cygnus Review

'Humorous, accessible, informative and inspirational... A delight to read'.

Kindred Spirit

ISBN: 0 7171 2985 3

From all good bookshops or directly from

www.gillmacmillan.ie